Certificate III in Business

Support personal wellbeing in the workplace

Core topic workbook

Linda Joel

—— A ——
FIVE SENSES
PUBLICATION

Five Senses Education Pty Ltd
2/195 Prospect Highway
Seven Hills 2147
New South Wales
Australia

Joel, Linda
Certificate III in Business
Support personal wellbeing in the workplace
Core topic workbook

ISBN 978-1-76032-500-8

Contents

A glossary of key words for assessment

Using the glossary will help students to understand what is expected in responses in examinations and assessment tasks.

Account:	Account for: state reasons for, report on. Give an account of: narrate a series of events or transactions
Analyse:	Identify components and the relationship between them; draw out and relate implications
Apply:	Use, utilise, employ in a particular situation
Appreciate;	Make a judgement about the value of
Assess:	Make a judgement of value, quality, outcomes, results or size
Calculate:	Ascertain/determine from given facts, figures or information
Clarify:	Make clear or plain
Classify:	Arrange or include in classes/categories
Compare:	Show how things are similar or different
Construct:	Make; build; put together items or arguments
Contrast:	Show how things are different or opposite
Critically: (analyse/ evaluate)	Add a degree or level of accuracy depth, knowledge and understanding, logic, questioning, reflection and quality to (analyse/evaluate)
Deduce:	Draw conclusions
Define:	State meaning and identify essential qualities
Demonstrate:	Show by example
Describe:	Provide characteristics and features
Discuss:	Identify issues and provide points for and/or against
Distinguish:	Recognise or note/indicate as being distinct or different from; to note differences between
Evaluate:	Make a judgement based on criteria; determine the value of

Examine:	Inquire into
Explain:	Relate cause and effect; make the relationships between things evident; provide why and/or how
Extract:	Choose relevant and/or appropriate details
Extrapolate:	Infer from what is known
Identify:	Recognise and name
Interpret:	Draw meaning from
Investigate:	Plan, inquire into and draw conclusions about
Justify:	Support an argument or conclusion
Outline:	Sketch in general terms; indicate the main features of
Predict:	Suggest what may happen based on available information
Propose:	Put forward (for example a point of view, idea, argument, suggestion) for consideration or action
Recall:	Present remembered ideas, facts or experiences
Recommend:	Provide reasons in favour
Recount:	Retell a series of events
Summarise:	Express, concisely, the relevant details
Synthesise:	Putting together various elements to make a whole

Chapter 1: Recognise factors that impact personal wellbeing

Short answers:

1. Define wellbeing. (2 marks)

_____

_____

_____

2. How does the social and economic environment impact personal wellbeing? (3 marks)

_____

_____

_____

_____

_____

3. What can a person do to achieve higher levels of wellbeing? (3 marks)

_____

_____

_____

_____

_____

_____

4. What is workplace wellbeing? (2 marks)

_____

_____

_____

5. What is a negative work culture? (2 marks)

_____

_____

_____

6. Identify three factors that can negatively impact worker wellbeing. (3 marks)

_____

_____

_____

7. Why is worker wellbeing so important for a business? (2 marks)

_____

_____

_____

8. What can happen when a worker's wellbeing is reduced? (3 marks)

_____

_____

_____

_____

_____

9. When do workers feel that they have no control over their personal wellbeing? (2 marks)

_____

_____

_____

Multiple choice:

1. What individual factor may impact wellbeing?
    a. Being in a stable loving relationship
    b. Having access to safe water and clean air
    c. Being able to afford a new car every couple of years
    d. Having access to good health services when needed

2. How can we achieve higher levels of wellbeing?
    a. By spending more hours at work
    b. Being optimistic and enjoying every day
    c. Micromanaging every aspect of our lives
    d. Having many shops nearby to spend money in

3. What is a reason why workers have little ability to make their own decisions?
   a. Workplace bullying
   b. Little professional learning
   c. Micromanaging supervisors
   d. High stress levels due to work demands

4. What is not optimal for a good work environment?
   a. Lack of privacy
   b. Air conditioning
   c. Realistic timeframes
   d. Separate lunch areas

5. What is an example of organisational change?
   a. Supporting workers
   b. Rearranging the furniture
   c. Restructuring and downsizing
   d. Changing the air conditioning temperature

6. How can reduced worker wellbeing impact business effectiveness?
   a. Reduce resignations
   b. Reduce mistakes and errors
   c. Reduce the number of grievances
   d. Reduce reputation of the business

7. Unclear roles are the result of a lack of understanding of what?
   a. Bullying
   b. Instruction
   c. Relationships
   d. Support

True or false?

8. The wellbeing of the worker is an increasingly relevant and necessary consideration in the modern workplace.

9. Level of income has no impact on mental health, only physical health.

10. Wellbeing is linked to safe communities with good street lighting.

11. Smoking and drinking affects the way we deal with life's challenges.

12. A dysfunctional family will help people cope with bad life experiences.

13. If workplace wellbeing is not high and not being addressed, then workers may feel satisfied and undervalued.

14. Unrealistic goals put on workers causes high stress levels.

15. Workplace air quality and temperature may affect worker wellbeing.

16. If there is little opportunity for professional learning, workers feel like they have the opportunity to progress at work.

17. Workplace bullying leads to increased depression.

18. Conflict between colleagues leads to negative workplace atmosphere.

19. Increased workloads are often the result of increased time limits for jobs.

20. Inflexible work hours indicate a lack of control workers have over their working conditions.

Write clues for the following completed crossword:

1 MORALE
2 OPPORTUNITIES
3 INSECURITY
4 SOCIALNETWORKS
5 GENETICS
6 ERGONOMICS
7 SOCIALLEVEL
8 SELFESTEEM
9 LACKOFSUPPORT
10 REWARDINGJOB
11 EXERCISE
12 TRUST
13 RESIGNATIONS
14 DISSATISFIED
15 CHANGE
16 OPTIMISTIC
17 HOBBIES
18 ABSENTEEISM
19 CONFLICT
20 WORKLOADS

Across:

1. ____

____

5. ____

____

6. ____

____

9. ____

____

12. _____

_____

14. _____

_____

17. _____

_____

18. _____

_____

20. _____

_____

Down:

2. _____

_____

3. _____

_____

4. _____

_____

7. _____

_____

8. _____

_____

10. _____

_____

11. _____

_____

13. _____

_____

15. _____

_____

16. _____

_____

19. _____

_____

Crossword:

Across:

2. This increases when a workspace is not optimal.

6. This is about how people feel and function.

11. Genetics plays a role in this.

13. This is compromised when worker wellbeing decreases. (2 words)

15. Progression is limited when there is a lack of these.

16. A human behaviour that affects wellbeing.

17. Workers feel like this when they are shown little gratitude for their work.

19. Often describes timeframes.

20. The greater the gap between these people, the greater the differences in health and wellbeing. (3 words)

Down:

1. This decreases when wellbeing dramatically reduces.

3. A source of stress in the workplace.

4. Some workers feel like this when there is not enough time to complete all the work tasks.

5. Workers feel they have a lack of control when left out of this process. (2 words)

7. Most workers have this type of work hours.

8. Little of this occurs in a negative work culture.

9. This type of health is better with higher incomes.

10. Reduced wellbeing results in this being higher.

12. This makes workers feel that their efforts are not noticed. (3 words)

14. Wellbeing decreases when this gets on top of you. (2 words)

18. Everybody needs a sense of this.

Extended response 1:

a) Outline how an individual's characteristics and behaviours impact wellbeing. (3 marks)

_____

_____

_____

_____

_____

b) Identify three typical responses in the workplace when a worker's wellbeing is reduced and outline how each one affects the business. (3 marks)

_____

_____

_____

_____

_____

_____

_____

_____

_____

_____

_____

c) Explain how workplace factors influence the wellbeing of the workers. (9 marks)

_____

_____

_____

_____

_____

_____

_____

_____

_____

_____

Support personal wellbeing in the workplace

Extended response 2:

Analyse the relationship between workplace factors that may impact on wellbeing and their possible resultant responses. (15 marks)

Your answer will be assessed on how well you:
- demonstrate knowledge and understanding relevant to the question
- communicate ideas and information using relevant workplace examples and industry terminology
- present a logical and cohesive response

_____

_____

_____

_____

_____

_____

_____

_____

_____

_____

_____

_____

_____

_____

_____

_____

_____

_____

_____

_____

_____

_____

_____

Support personal wellbeing in the workplace   © Five Senses Education Pty Ltd and Linda Joel

Chapter 2: Plan communication with supervisor

Short answers:

1. Define communication. (2 marks)

_____

_____

2. Identify the basic elements of the communication cycle. (8 marks)

_____

_____

_____

_____

_____

_____

_____

_____

3. What is expressive speaking? (2 marks)

_____

_____

4. What is empathetic listening? (2 marks)

_____

_____

_____

5. Why is it important for a supervisor to show sensitivity to feelings? (2 marks)

_____

_____

6. Why is it best to schedule a face-to-face meeting with a supervisor to talk about wellbeing issues? (2 marks)

_____

_____

_____

7. Why is it important for a worker to remain calm during meetings with a supervisor about wellbeing issues? (2 marks)

_____

_____

_____

8. What are advantages of flexible work hours? (2 marks)

_____

_____

_____

9. What should a worker do if the response from the supervisor is negative? (2 marks)

_____

_____

_____

Multiple choice:

1. What is encoding?
   a. How the message is written or stated
   b. The person deciphering the message
   c. Sending the message to another person
   d. How the message is interpreted and understood

2. What is the most appropriate method of communicating with a supervisor about wellbeing issues?
   a. Emails
   b. Over the phone
   c. Verbally in any meeting
   d. Verbally on a one-to-one basis

3. What is expressive speaking?
    a. Using hands as you speak
    b. Showing emotions while speaking
    c. Being able to fully explain the situation
    d. Using colourful language to get point across

4. Who should show sensitivity to feelings when discussing wellbeing?
    a. Colleagues
    b. Supervisor
    c. Team leader
    d. Workers

5. Why would a supervisor use facial expressions in discussions about wellbeing?
    a. It is to show empathy to put the worker at ease
    b. It is quicker and easier to get the point across to the worker
    c. It is easier to use facial expressions than verbal expressions
    d. It is expected of supervisors to use a lot of non-verbal language

6. What is a downside to meetings to discuss wellbeing?
    a. Feelings can be hurt
    b. Emotions are disregarded
    c. Worker loses concentration
    d. Not enough time to cover everything

7. Why should a worker take a plan into a meeting with him/her?
    a. To keep to the agenda
    b. In case their emotions get carried away
    c. So they don't leave anything details out
    d. So they look like they have come prepared

8. Why is an advantage of rearranging the work schedule?
    a. Fewer interruptions to work
    b. To improve the work-life balance
    c. So more people can share the workload
    d. So everyone can work from home once a week

True or false?

9. The quality of communication will depend on the level of perceive fairness.

10. Supervisors need to be judgemental so that workers feel they can ask for help when needed.

11. Communication is the process of exchanging information.

12. The channel of communication is the means by which the message is sent.

13. Decoding is how the message is written or stated, considering language barriers.

14. Response is the acknowledgement of or reaction to the message.

15. Feedback is always negative.

16. A worker may first send an email requesting a meeting with his/her supervisor.

17. The first email about wellbeing should include a lot of detail for discussion.

18. The relationship between a worker and supervisor is generally closer in a smaller business.

19. Details discussed in meetings should be shared with other workers in case they have the same concerns.

20. The supervisor should listen without interrupting to show they care about the worker and his/her problems.

21. If a worker isn't keen on oversharing details, then it is alright to talk in general terms about stress, anxiety or depression.

22. Hope and anxiety are positive emotions.

23. The display of emotions is often more likely to make the problem worse than to help solve it.

24. It is always important to be concise and straightforward when discussing wellbeing issues.

25. It is a good idea for the worker to take a list of suggestions that could be discussed.

26. Introducing flexible work hours can increase the stress in the workplace.

27. Working from home can increase productivity as there are fewer interruptions.

28. If the supervisor's response is negative, accept the advice and leave the meeting.

29. Clarifying questions can be asked if the response is negative.

30. The worker could ask for some leave to look after their health.

Write clues for the following completed crossword:

Across:

2. _____

_____

5. _____

_____

8. _____

_____

10. _____

_____

14. _____

_____

16. _____

_____

17. _____

_____

Down:

1. _____

_____

3. _____

_____

4. _____

_____

6. _____

_____

7. _____

_____

9. _____

_____

11. _____

_____

12. _____

_____

13. _____

_____

15. _____

_____

Crossword:

Across:

1. Workers should remain like this in meetings to keep their feelings in check.
6. The quality of communication will depend on levels of this. (2 words)
9. How a message is written or stated.
11. Showing kindness and caring.
13. Positive outcome of flexible working hours. (2 words)
14. Refers to the subject matter of meetings about wellbeing. (2 words)
15. This should be included in an initial email to set up a meeting about wellbeing issues. (2 words)
17. The best way to discuss wellbeing.
18. It is important to display this with emotions.
19. To be able to fully explain a situation.

Down:

2. A negative emotion.
3. It is important to always be this during meetings.
4. A positive emotion.
5. Reaction to a message.
7. How a message is understood by the receiver.
8. Type of business where the relationship between staff and supervisors is relatively close.
9. To listen without interrupting.
10. This should not occur when listening to someone.
12. Emotional responses will set this for the entire meeting.
16. When talking to someone about wellbeing helps.

Extended response:

Explain how to plan communication with a supervisor about declining wellbeing.

(15 marks)

Your answer will be assessed on how well you:
- demonstrate knowledge and understanding relevant to the question
- communicate ideas and information using relevant workplace examples and industry terminology
- present a logical and cohesive response

_____

_____

_____

_____

_____

_____

_____

_____

_____

_____

_____

_____

_____

_____

_____

_____

_____

_____

_____

_____

_____

_____

_____

Support personal wellbeing in the workplace

Chapter 3: Communicate with supervisor

1. What should be taken into account when scheduling a meeting with a supervisor? (1 mark)

    _____

    _____

2. When would a supervisor not be able to sit down for a discussion with a worker?   (2 marks)

    _____

    _____

3. What times should be avoided when trying to set up a meeting time?   (3 marks)

    _____

    _____

    _____

4. What could be included on a prepared list for discussion during the meeting?   (3 marks)

    _____

    _____

    _____

5. How should you act during a meeting?   (3 marks)

    _____

    _____

    _____

    _____

    _____

6. How do you know if the meeting has been a success?   (3 marks)

    _____

    _____

    _____

    _____

    _____

    _____

Multiple choice:

1. What should be taken into account when setting up a meeting with a supervisor?
   a. What time they have lunch
   b. Where they have their lunch
   c. Any time constraints they may have
   d. Whether they have to rush off to a meeting

2. When is a good time to set up a meeting with a supervisor?
   a. Early in the morning
   b. Late in the afternoon
   c. In the middle of the day
   d. In the middle of the afternoon

3. How can you prepare for a meeting with a supervisor?
   a. Take a list of demands with you
   b. Have a practice run with a colleague
   c. Write a list of issues affecting your wellbeing
   d. Take a colleague with you to explain the situation

4. What should you do during a meeting with a supervisor?
   a. Argue a point
   b. Listen with an open mind
   c. Focus on individual people
   d. Show no respect towards your colleagues

5. What is the first step in changing attitudes and behaviour in a workplace that badly affect the wellbeing of workers?
   a. Raise the awareness of the supervisor about the problem
   b. Hold a meeting of all workers to see who is affected the most
   c. Down tools and refuse to continue working until problem is fixed
   d. Have a meeting to come up with strategies to help solve the problem

True or false?

6. An email should be sent to a supervisor to set up a time for a meeting.

7. 9 am is a good time for a meeting before everyone gets too tired.

8. Supervisors who have an open door for communication are usually the most approachable.

9. Taking a list to a meeting ensures that details will be left out.

10. Always give just one solution to fix a problem.

11. Manage your emotions, language and behaviour in meetings with a supervisor.

12. A supervisor must be convinced of the importance of the need for change to occur.

13. Workers must facilitate the change for a happier workplace.

14. If a supervisor brushes it off, then it may take some time to see if the communication was effective or not, depending on what action the supervisor consequently takes.

15. Effective communication would lead to a discussion about possible paths of action.

Write clues for the following completed crossword:

Across:

5. _____

_____

6. _____

_____

8. _____

_____

9. _____

_____

11. _____

_____

12. _____

_____

Down:

1. _____

_____

2. _____

_____

3. _____

_____

4. _____

_____

7. _____

_____

10. _____

_____

Crossword:

Across:

2. This must be managed when talking to a supervisor about wellbeing issues.

7. A good time to schedule a meeting with a supervisor.

8. Sometimes a supervisor is under the pressure of one of these and can't schedule a meeting.

10. Never enter into one of these during a discussion with a supervisor.

13. An often-used phrase spoken by a supervisor when they haven't got time to deal with something. (4 words)

14. The result of finding a solution to a wellbeing problem. (2 words)

15. You need one of these to accept alternative viewpoints. (2 words)

16. You send one of these to set up a meeting time.

Down:

1. A topic often discussed in meetings with supervisors.

3. In meetings, it is important to focus on problems and not these. (2 words)

4. Supervisors should show this in order to solve a problem about wellbeing.

5. Supervisors often have to be convinced of this. (3 words)

6. Always take one of these into a meeting so you don't forget any details.

9. You must always be this in meetings.

11. Supervisors are under this to solve problems.

12. Supervisors with an open-door policy are always this.

Chapter 4: Investigate available wellbeing resources

1. What does it take to develop an effective workplace wellbeing program? (2 marks)

_____

_____

2. What constitutes flexible working hours and what are its benefits? (4 marks)

_____

_____

_____

_____

_____

3. Outline the pros and cons of open plan and closed working environments. (4 marks)

_____

_____

_____

_____

4. What are the benefits of encouraging open communication between workers and management? (2 marks)

_____

_____

_____

5. What are the benefits of rewarding staff for good work? (2 marks)

_____

_____

6. Identify the rewards that could be given to workers for good work. (3 marks)

_____

_____

_____

_____

_____

7. What are the risks of sitting for long periods of time? (2 marks)

_____

_____

8. What changes can be made so there is more natural light in an office? (2 marks)

_____

_____

_____

9. Identify some changes that can be made at little or no cost to increase wellbeing. (2 marks)

_____

_____

_____

10. Why should records be kept of programs implemented to increase wellbeing? (2 marks)

_____

_____

_____

11. What is the difference between an action plan and a promotional plan? (2 marks)

_____

_____

_____

_____

Multiple choice:

1. On what will strategies to improve worker wellbeing ultimately depend?
   a. The size and type of business
   b. If management makes the suggestions
   c. If there is money available to support it
   d. Whether everyone is willing to participate

2. What needs to be looked at first before any programs can be introduced to improve wellbeing?
   a. Time restraints
   b. Work-related stress
   c. Worker participation
   d. Support from management

3. What happens when workers don't communicate with each other?
   a. Conflict reduces
   b. No problems arise
   c. Productivity increases
   d. Things can go wrong fast

4. What is a benefit of devising a fitness challenge for workers?
   a. Promotes fun and friendly competition
   b. Adds exercise without sacrificing productivity
   c. Workers can use the gym anytime they want to
   d. Workers have to work with people they don't normally work with

5. What is the minimum number of hours a worker should stand for an hour to prevent health problems?
   a. 10 minutes
   b. 15 minutes
   c. 20 minutes
   d. 25 minutes

6. How can a worker add movement and exercise into the work day?
   a. Walk to work
   b. Use a sit/stand desk
   c. Have walking meetings
   d. Do a yoga class at lunchtime

7. What is a benefit of encouraging everyone to not eat lunch at their desk?
   a. Keeps cleaning up to one room
   b. Can play darts or table tennis during lunch
   c. Helps to clear the mind for the afternoon work
   d. Less chance of eating junk food as everyone is watching

8. What kind of activity encourages workers to communicate with each other?
   a. Walking meetings
   b. Team bonding sessions
   c. Providing a free fruit bowl
   d. Playing darts at lunchtime

9. After establishing a committee, what is the next step to create a workplace health and wellbeing program?
    a. Devise an action plan of strategies
    b. Talk to workers about what should be done
    c. Conduct a formal survey about needs and interests of workers
    d. Talk to everyone from management down about what should be done

10. What will determine the success of a new program?
    a. How often the program runs
    b. Whether the boss participates or not
    c. How well the objectives are communicated
    d. How much money is spent on providing resources

11. What is NOT included in an activity and event log?
    a. List of activities run
    b. Records of participation
    c. An evaluation of each activity
    d. Who is responsible for each activity

True or false?

12. Workplace wellbeing should have a clear focus, strong drive and measurable outcomes.

13. To be successful, any new policy about wellbeing must reach and be absorbed by every person in every department and at every level of management.

14. Flexible working hours are only successful if the workers trust the boss to pay them correctly.

15. The Covid-19 pandemic showed that workers became a lot more productive when working from home.

16. Open plan offices make building relationships more difficult as there is a lack of privacy.

17. An open-door policy encourages supervisors to speak more often to the boss.

18. Open communication can increase conflict while promoting productivity.

19. Most employees feel that recognition for good work makes coming to work worthwhile.

20. Working in teams inspires individuals to push themselves harder than they would on their own.

21. A sit/stand desk can also prevent neck, shoulder and leg pain.

22. Allowing pets in the workplace increases collective stress and decreases productivity.

23. Exposure to natural light affects workers' quality of life, vitality and night time function.

24. Getting away from the desk for lunch helps to clear the mind and increases afternoon productivity.

25. Providing a free fruit bowl makes it easier to snack healthily instead of going for junk food.

26. A work sport team encourages teamwork and better relationships between workers.

27. Competitions between departments for a bit of fun at work helps boost staff morale.

28. The first step before creating a workplace health and wellbeing program is to survey management for ideas.

29. Small businesses who know their staff better can purchase more resources to implement programs.

30. Larger workplaces could make physical changes to promote wellbeing, like providing a games room or gym for workers.

31. There should be some variety of activities to cater for individual differences.

32. A plan will be successful if it caters for the majority of the workers' interests.

33. It is important to document the progress for initiating and implementing the action plan.

34. The action plan monitors and evaluates each activity.

35. Keeping records will assist future planning of activities.

Write clues for the following completed crossword:

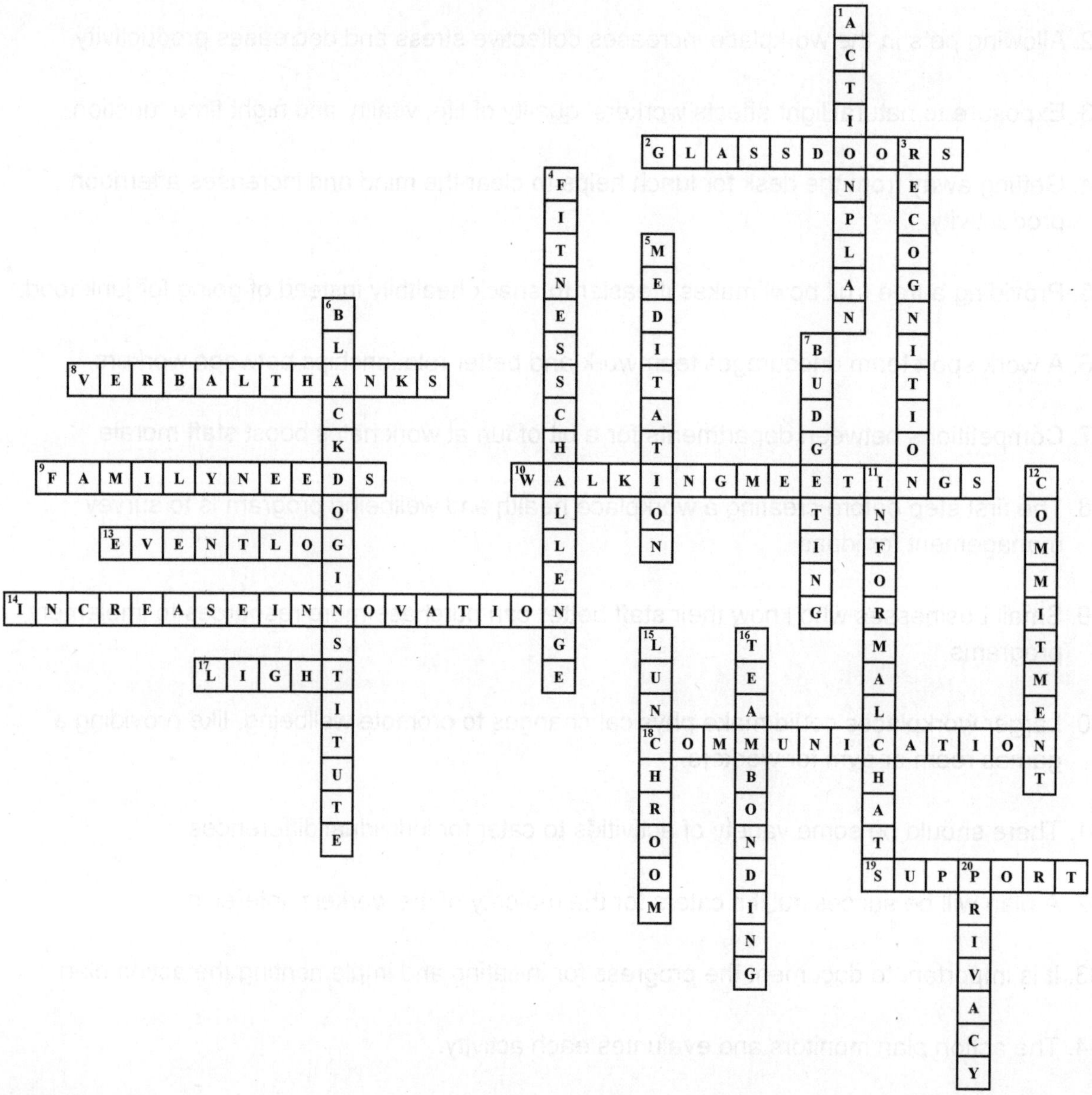
1 ACTIONPLAN
2 GLASSDOORS
3 RECOGNITION
4 FITNESSCHALLENGE
5 MEDITATION
6 BLACKDOGINSTITUTE
7 BUDGETING
8 VERBALTHANKS
9 FAMILYNEEDS
10 WALKINGMEETINGS
11 INFORMALCHAT
12 COMMITMENT
13 EVENTLOG
14 INCREASEINNOVATION
15 LUNCHROOM
16 TEAMBONDING
17 LIGHT
18 COMMUNICATION
19 SUPPORT
20 PRIVACY

Across:

2. ____

8. ____

9. ____

10. ____

13. _____

_____

14. _____

_____

17. _____

_____

18. _____

_____

19. _____

_____

Down:

1. _____

_____

3. _____

_____

4. _____

_____

5. _____

_____

6. _____

_____

7. _____

_____

11. _____

_____

12. _____

_____

15. _____

_____

16. _____

_____

20. _____

_____

Crossword:

Across:

4. These unlock the spirit of fun.

5. These can be changed to fit around family needs. (2 words)

7. All workplace wellbeing programs should have these. (2 words)

9. This should be established before creating a wellbeing program.

10. This will catch a problem before it arises. (2 words)

11. Ergonomic furniture of today. (3 words)

13. This should occur at the end of every activity.

14. This should be addressed before implementing new wellbeing programs. (3 words)

15. A work sport team supports this. (2 words)

17. This encourages friendly competition. (2 words)

Down:

1. Eating lunch away from the desk will increase this in the afternoon.

2. "Employee of the Month" is an example of this. (2 words)

3. This is required when developing an effective workplace wellbeing program.

6. A website that lists tools and resources available online for business regarding wellbeing. (2 words)

8. An example of a team bonding day. (2 words)

12. This is necessary for a walking meeting. (2 words)

16. These must still be met when workers work from home.

18. These people must participate if a wellbeing program is to be successful.

Extended response:

Identify and review strategies that can be introduced to improve workplace wellbeing.

(15 marks)

Your answer will be assessed on how well you:
- demonstrate knowledge and understanding relevant to the question
- communicate ideas and information using relevant workplace examples and industry terminology
- present a logical and cohesive response

_____

_____

_____

_____

_____

_____

_____

_____

_____

_____

_____

_____

_____

_____

_____

_____

_____

_____

_____

_____

_____

_____

_____

Support personal wellbeing in the workplace

Chapter 5: Assessment tasks to provide evidence of ability and demonstration of knowledge of topic

Each student must provide evidence of the ability to:

- develop a plan for communication with supervisor
- develop a plan to communicate with supervisor, which includes:
    - factors that may impact on own wellbeing, both positively and negatively
    - appropriate style of communication
    - appropriate method of communication
    - strategy to deal with negative response
- identify and access one formal and one informal wellbeing resource

Each student must also demonstrate knowledge of:

- common personal and workplace factors that may impact on wellbeing
- advantages and disadvantages of different communication styles, including:
    - passive
    - assertive
    - aggressive
- methods for communicating with a supervisor
- key features of Employee Assistance Programs (EAPs)
- common workplace resources for addressing wellbeing

Instructions:

These tasks are to be completed by each individual student and should be submitted on your own paper for marking. Submitted answers will be marked as competent or not yet competent. Any task that is deemed not yet competent must be reviewed, updated and resubmitted until it has been deemed competent.

Task 1:

a. For each of the following communication styles, write a definition, identify advantages and disadvantages and give at least one example of how you would use each one when speaking to your supervisor:

- Assertive
- Aggressive
- Passive
- Passive-aggressive
- Manipulative
- Submissive
- Direct
- Indirect

b. Outline the best methods of communicating with a supervisor, using examples for a range of scenarios.

Task 2:

Identify the common personal and workplace factors that may impact on worker wellbeing. Explain the effects each of these factors can have on a worker's mental and physical health as well as his/her performance at work.

Task 3:

What is an Employee Assistance Program (EAP)? Outline the key features of an EAP and the benefits workers and/or their families may derive from this type of support.

Task 4:

Visit at least 3 different local businesses. Write a brief report on how they address wellbeing in their workplace.

Task 5:

You are having a difficult time with your work-life balance. As a result, your stress levels have been rising lately and you feel that you are not performing to your full potential. You wish to speak to your supervisor about it.

a. Explain the steps you would take to set up this meeting.

b. Develop a plan to communicate with your supervisor, including:
    - The factors that have been impacting on your work-life balance (both negative and positive)
    - The stye of communication you would use
    - The method of communication you would use
    - Strategies you would use if the response was negative

Task 6:

Go to the following website for the Black Dog Institute:
https://www.blackdoginstitute.org.au/resources-support/wellbeing/workplace-wellbeing/

Assess the effectiveness of the information on this website in assisting businesses in becoming mentally healthy workplaces.

Chapter 6: Marking guidelines and suggested answers

Note: no suggested answers are given for the completed crosswords as answers will vary for each student.

Chapter 1:

1. Wellbeing is defined as being a state of being comfortable, healthy and happy; how people feel and function on both a personal level and on a social level, including at work, and how they evaluate their lives as a whole.

Marks	Criteria
2	• Detailed definition of wellbeing
1	• Mentions at least one point about wellbeing

2. The social and economic environment includes:
   - The level of income and social status: higher income is associated with higher social status and better health
   - Having good social networks of family and friends for support
   - Having access to good health services

Marks	Criteria
3	• Detailed explanation of how the social and economic environment affects wellbeing
2	• Good explanation of how the social and economic environment affects wellbeing
1	• Mentions at least one relevant point

3. In order to achieve higher levels of wellbeing, it is important to:
   - Develop and maintain strong relationships with family and friends
   - Find a job that is rewarding and not just for the highest pay packet
   - Get involved in activities, organisations or clubs that interest you
   - Set achievable goals and work towards them
   - Eat nutritious food and enjoy a balance diet
   - Regularly make time for social activities
   - Be optimistic and enjoy every day
   - Exercise regularly

Marks	Criteria
3	• Detailed explanation of a range of things a person can do to achieve higher levels of wellbeing
2	• Good explanation of a number of things a person can do to achieve higher levels of wellbeing
1	• Mentions at least one thing a person can do to achieve higher levels of wellbeing

4. Workplace wellbeing relates to how workers feel about themselves at work, especially how satisfied and engaged they are with their work.

Marks	Criteria
2	• Detailed definition of workplace wellbeing
1	• Mentions at least one point about workplace wellbeing

5. Negative work culture: little help is provided to struggling workers; little trust is put in workers; workers are shown little gratitude for the good things but are blamed quickly if things go wrong; very little collaboration occurs as direction comes from micromanaging bosses

Marks	Criteria
2	• Detailed explanation of negative workplace culture
1	• Mentions at least one point about negative workplace culture

6. Other factors that can negatively impact worker wellbeing:
   • Micromanaging bosses
   • High stress levels due to unrealistic goals
   • Badly designed work environment
   • Lack of opportunity for training or promotion
   • Workplace bullying
   • Organisational change
   • Lack of recognition and reward
   • Lack of support

Marks	Criteria
3	• Identifies three other factors that can negatively impact worker wellbeing
2	• Identifies two other factors that can negatively impact worker wellbeing
1	• Identifies one other factor that can negatively impact worker wellbeing

7. Wellbeing is a major factor in quality, performance, productivity of workers and therefore business effectiveness and profit.

Marks	Criteria
2	• Detailed explanation of why worker wellbeing is important for a business
1	• Mentions at least one relevant point

8. Reduced workers wellbeing can result in:
- Reduced productivity
- Increased mistakes and errors
- Poorer quality customer service
- Higher levels of sickness and absenteeism
- Low morale and negative workplace atmosphere
- Conflict with colleagues and supervisors/managers
- Increased number of grievance and disciplinary incidents
- Poor employer reputation among staff, customers, and potential new recruits
- Higher rates of resignations and job terminations, causing increased rates of staff turnover

Marks	Criteria
3	• Detailed explanation of what can happen when worker wellbeing is reduced
2	• Good explanation of what can happen when worker wellbeing is reduced
1	• Mentions at least one relevant point

9. Workers feel they have no control over their personal wellbeing when:

- Change occurs at work
- Relationships break down
- Roles are unclear
- High demands are placed on workers
- Lack of support
- Lack of control over own job

Marks	Criteria
2	• Detailed explanation of when workers have no control over their personal wellbeing
1	• Mentions at least one relevant point

Multiple choice and true/false:

1	2	3	4	5	6	7	8	9	10
a	b	c	a	c	d	b	T	F	T
11	12	13	14	15	16	17	18	19	20
T	F	F	T	T	F	T	T	F	T

Crossword:

Across:
2. NOISE
6. WELLBEING
11. HEALTHINESS
13. CUSTOMER SERVICE
15. OPPORTUNITIES
16. SLEEP
17. UNDERVALUED
19. UNREALISTIC
20. RICH AND POOR

Down:
1. MORAL
3. BULLYING
4. OVERWHELM
5. DECISION
7. INFLEXIBLE
8. COLLABORATION
9. PHYSICAL
10. RESIGNATION
12. LACK OFF REWARD
14. WORKLOADS
18. BELONGING

Extended response 1:

1. Answer could include:
   - Genetics: genetics plays a role in determining a person's lifespan, healthiness and likelihood of developing certain illness which can result in higher levels of stress and anticipation
   - Personal behaviours: smoking, drinking, exercising, balanced eating, getting enough sleep and pursuing hobbies and interests, can affect our health and how we deal with stress and life's challenges
   - Stable loving relationships/families: important for wellbeing whereas a partnership breakup or a dysfunctional family will have a devastating effect on how someone copes with all life experiences at that time
   - Being optimistic, setting realistic and achievable goals and being able to adapt to change
   - Having a sense of belonging

Marks	Criteria
3	• Demonstrates a sound understanding of an individual's characteristics and behaviours and their impact on wellbeing
2	• Demonstrates a some understanding of an individual's characteristics and behaviours and their impact on wellbeing
1	• Provides some relevant information

2. Answer may include:
   The typical responses in the workplace when a worker's wellbeing is reduced include:
   - Reduced productivity: increased costs, production may not keep up with demand, lose customers
   - Increased mistakes and errors: lost time, increased costs, disgruntled customers, more returned goods, damaged business reputation
   - Poorer quality customer service: lose customers, poor business reputation
   - Higher levels of sickness and absenteeism: affects productivity and output
   - Low morale and negative workplace atmosphere: workers not working to full potential, declined output, more mistakes being made
   - Conflict with colleagues and supervisors/managers: production slows or stops, increased costs, output not keeping up with demand, lose customers
   - Increased number of grievance and disciplinary incidents: higher turnover of staff, increased costs of recruitment of new staff, time and money lost
   - Poor employer reputation among staff, customers, and potential new recruits: difficult to recruit staff, increased costs, higher training costs, lose customers or markets
   - Higher rates of resignations and job terminations, causing increased rates of staff turnover: increased costs, may not keep up with demand, lose customers

Marks	Criteria
3	• Demonstrates a sound understanding of how responses to reduction in worker wellbeing affects the business
2	• Demonstrates a some understanding of how responses to reduction in worker wellbeing affects the business
1	• Provides some relevant information

3. Answer could include:
Workplace factors that may impact on wellbeing include:
- Micromanaging bosses: workers have no autonomy or ability to make their own decisions as their bosses micromanage everything, which leads to low levels of morale and job dissatisfaction
- High stress levels: often due to unrealistic goals put on workers so they feel they can never achieve what is expected of them
- Negative work culture: little help is provided to struggling workers; little trust is put in workers; workers are shown little gratitude for the good things but are blamed quickly if things go wrong; very little collaboration occurs as direction comes from micromanaging bosses
- Design of workspaces is not optimal: this includes indoor air quality and temperature, access to daylight, poor lighting, glare, noise control, ergonomics, office layout, lack of privacy, no separate space for eating lunch or having meetings
- Lack of opportunity: little opportunity for professional learning so workers feel like they have little or no opportunity to progress at work
- Workplace bullying: interpersonal relationships are often the source of workplace problems and stress, resulting in depression and lack of self-worth
- Organisational change: restructuring and downsizing can lead to increased stress and feelings of insecurity, especially if there is a lack of communication from management about the process to be followed
- Lack of recognition and reward: workers sometimes feel that their efforts go unnoticed
- Lack of support: particularly when overwhelmed by the amount or type of tasks that workers have to complete, sometimes with unrealistic timeframes

Marks	Criteria
8-9	• Demonstrates an extensive knowledge of how workplace factors influence worker wellbeing
6-7	• Demonstrates a thorough knowledge of how workplace factors influence worker wellbeing
4-5	• Demonstrates some knowledge of how workplace factors influence worker wellbeing
2-3	• Demonstrates some knowledge of worker wellbeing
1	• Provides some relevant information

Extended response 2:

Analyse: Identify components and the relationship between them; draw out and relate implications

Workplace factors: See suggested answers to Extended response 1, part c above.

Possible resultant responses: see suggested answers to Extended response 1, part b above.

Marks	Criteria
13-15	• Demonstrates an extensive knowledge and understanding of workplace factors that may impact on wellbeing and their possible resultant responses • Clearly explains the relationship between workplace factors that may impact on wellbeing and their possible resultant responses • Communicates ideas and information using relevant workplace examples and industry terminology • Presents a logical and cohesive response
10-12	• Demonstrates a sound knowledge and understanding of workplace factors that may impact on wellbeing and their possible resultant responses • Explains the relationship between workplace factors that may impact on wellbeing and their possible resultant responses. • Communicates using relevant workplace examples and industry terminology • Presents a logical response
7-9	• Demonstrates some knowledge and understanding of workplace factors that may impact on wellbeing and their possible resultant responses • Shows some relationship between workplace factors that may impact on wellbeing and their possible resultant responses. • Communicates using some workplace examples and industry terminology • Demonstrates some organisation in presenting information
4-6	• Demonstrates basic knowledge and/or understanding of wellbeing in the workplace • Uses some industry terminology
1-3	• Provides some relevant information

Chapter 2:

1. Communication is the process of exchanging information, both verbally, non-verbally, or in writing.

Marks	Criteria
2	• Detailed definition of communication
1	• Mentions at least one relevant point

2. The basic elements of the communication cycle include:
   - Sender: the person sending the message
   - Message: the information the sender wants to convey
   - Encoding: how the message is written or stated, considering language barriers and cultural differences
   - Channel: the means by which the message is sent (verbal, written, electronic)
   - Receiver: the person who is receiving the message
   - Decoding: how the message is interpreted and understood by the receiver
   - Response: acknowledgement of or reaction to the message
   - Feedback: good or bad comments given to the sender by the recipient

Marks	Criteria
8	• Identifies eight elements of the communication cycle
7	• Identifies seven elements of the communication cycle
6	• Identifies six elements of the communication cycle
5	• Identifies five elements of the communication cycle
4	• Identifies four elements of the communication cycle
3	• Identifies three elements of the communication cycle
2	• Identifies two elements of the communication cycle
1	• Identifies one element of the communication cycle

3. Expressive speaking is being able to explain the situation so the supervisor fully understands the problem.

Marks	Criteria
2	• Detailed definition of expressive speaking
1	• Mentions at least one relevant point

4. Empathetic listening is listening without interrupting, being mindful of the emotional content being delivered, as well as the literal meaning of the words to show that you care about the person speaking and their problems.

Marks	Criteria
2	• Detailed definition of empathetic listening
1	• Mentions at least one relevant point

5. The supervisor should be sensitive to feelings to show kindness and be caring so that they show the worker that they are aware of their needs and are willing to help them.

Marks	Criteria
2	• Detailed description of why it is important to show sensitivity to feelings
1	• Mentions at least one relevant point

6. Because of the personal nature of wellbeing, it is best to schedule a face-to-face meeting with a supervisor. The supervisor's response, tone of voice and expressions can put the worker at ease so the worker feels it hasn't been a waste of time.

Marks	Criteria
2	• Detailed description of why it is best to have face-to-face meetings about wellbeing issues
1	• Mentions at least one relevant point

7. A worker should remain calm during meetings about wellbeing as emotions can run high and feelings can be hurt. The worker may feel frustrated, angry, or hurt by the response of their supervisor, but the display of these emotions is often more likely to make the problem worse than to help solve it.

Marks	Criteria
2	• Detailed description of why it is best to remain calm during meetings about wellbeing
1	• Mentions at least one relevant point

8. Flexible work hours enable a worker to enjoy a better work-life balance to reduce stress in the workplace and increase productivity.

Marks	Criteria
2	• Detailed description of the benefits of flexible work hours
1	• Mentions at least one relevant point

9. If the response from the supervisor is negative, the worker should ask clarifying questions about what can be done to fix the situation or ask for some leave to look after their health.

Marks	Criteria
2	• Detailed description of what to do if the response is negative
1	• Mentions at least one relevant point

Multiple choice and true/false:

1	2	3	4	5	6	7	8	9	10
a	d	c	b	a	a	c	c	T	F
11	**12**	**13**	**14**	**15**	**16**	**17**	**18**	**19**	**20**
T	T	F	T	F	T	F	T	F	T
21	**22**	**23**	**24**	**25**	**26**	**27**	**28**	**29**	**30**
T	F	T	T	T	F	T	F	T	T

Crossword:

Across:

1. CALM
6. PERCEIVED
7. DECODING
9. ENCODING
11. SENSITIVE
13. REDUCESTRESS
14. PERSONALNATURE
15. LITTLEDETAIL
17. OPENLY
18. CONTROL
19. EXPRESSIVE

Down:

2. ANXIETY
3. STRAIGHTFORWARD
4. OPTIMISM
5. RESPONSE
8. SMALL
10. INTERRUPTIONS
12. TOE
16. THERAPEUTIC
EMPATHETIC

Extended response:

Answer should include information about the following:

- When you feel you should speak to your supervisor
- How to set up a meeting
- Elements of the communication cycle: a description of the most relevant
- Communication skills
- Strategies to use during the discussion
- Suggestions that could help the situation
- How to prepare for a negative response

Marks	Criteria
13-15	• Demonstrates an extensive knowledge and understanding of wellbeing and the ability to communicate with others • Communicates ideas and information using relevant workplace examples and industry terminology • Presents a logical and cohesive response
10-12	• Demonstrates a sound knowledge and understanding of wellbeing and the ability to communicate with others • Communicates using relevant workplace examples and industry terminology • Presents a logical response
7-9	• Demonstrates some knowledge and understanding of wellbeing and the ability to communicate with others • Communicates using some workplace examples and industry terminology • Demonstrates some organisation in presenting information
4-6	• Demonstrates basic knowledge and/or understanding of wellbeing and communication • Uses some industry terminology
1-3	• Provides some relevant information

Chapter 3:

1. Time constraints of the supervisor should be taken into account.

Marks	Criteria
1	• Correctly identifies time constraints

2. A supervisor would not be able to sit down for a meeting when:
   - Under pressure to meet a deadline
   - Resolve an important problem

Marks	Criteria
2	• Mentions two reasons
1	• Mentions one reason

3. Times that should be avoided are:
   - 9am when staff are just arriving and the supervisor must make sure that everything is prepared for the day ahead
   - Lunchtime
   - Around 5-5.30pm, when the supervisor may be heading out the door to go home or is busy attending to problems that have arisen during the day

Marks	Criteria
3	• Mentions three times to be avoided
2	• Mentions two times to be avoided
1	• Mentions one time to be avoided

4. A prepared list could include:
   - Issues affecting your wellbeing
   - Questions
   - Possible solutions

Marks	Criteria
3	• Mentions three items
2	• Mentions two items
1	• Mentions one item

5. During a meeting, you should be honest, display respect, listen with an open mind, do not enter into a debate, focus on issues not people, manage your emotions and behaviour.

Marks	Criteria
3	• Detailed description of how you should act in a meeting
2	• Good description of how you should act in a meeting
1	• Mentions at least one relevant point

6. You know if the meeting has been a success if:
   • The supervisor shows empathy
   • You are not brushed off
   • The supervisor is willing to do something about the problem
   • The supervisor follows through with promised action

Marks	Criteria
3	• Detailed description of how you know if the meeting has been a success
2	• Good description of how you know if the meeting has been a success
1	• Mentions at least one relevant point

Multiple choice and true/false:

1	2	3	4	5	6	7	8	9	10
d	c	c	b	a	T	F	T	F	F

11	12	13	14	15					
T	T	F	F	T					

Crossword:

Chapter 4:

1. Developing an effective workplace wellbeing program takes time, commitment and strategy, and will need support from management.

Marks	Criteria
2	• Detailed description of what it takes to develop an effective wellbeing program
1	• Mentions at least one relevant point

2. Flexible work hours allow the worker to determine the actual hours spent in the workplace as long as they still attend for eight hours. For example, instead of working 9am to 5pm, a worker could work 7am to 3pm or 8am to 4pm. Workers could also work from home for one or two days a week. Flexible working hours at the office allows workers to alter their work habits to fit family needs (like school drop-offs and pick-ups) while at the same time, avoid peak travel periods, so spending less time in traffic.

Marks	Criteria
4	• Detailed explanation of both what constitutes flexible work hours and its benefits
3	• Good explanation of both what constitutes flexible work hours and its benefits
2	• Good explanation of either what constitutes flexible work hours or its benefits
1	• Mentions at least one relevant point

3. Open plan offices lack privacy but foster a sociable environment and open culture, which is particularly helpful for teamwork, whereas closed offices are more private but are often lonely, and make building relationships more difficult.

Marks	Criteria
4	• Detailed outline of pros and cons of open plan and closed working environments
3	• Good explanation of pros and cons of open plan and closed working environments
2	• Good explanation of either pros and cons of open plan or closed working environments
1	• Mentions at least one relevant point

4. Open communication reduces office conflict, catches problems before they arise, promotes productivity, encourages the sharing of ideas and increases innovation, and helps to keep employees around longer

Marks	Criteria
2	• Detailed explanation of the benefits of open communication
1	• Mentions at least one relevant point

5. Most employees feel that recognition for good work makes coming to work worthwhile and it makes them happier both at work and at home.

Marks	Criteria
2	• Detailed explanation of the benefits of rewarding staff for good work
1	• Mentions at least one relevant point

6. Recognition could come in the form of:
   - receiving verbal thanks from colleagues, supervisor or the boss
   - a hand-written note from a colleague, supervisor or boss recognising the effort that has gone into a job or for their achievements
   - verbal recognition/praise in a staff meeting
   - a physical award like "Employee of the Month/Year"
   - a pay rise or extra time off work
   - flowers or a gift

Marks	Criteria
3	• Identifies a range of rewards
2	• Identifies more than one reward
1	• Identifies at least one reward

7. Sitting is considered to be the new smoking, putting workers at increased risk of obesity, diabetes, heart disease, a variety of cancers and early death, as well as neck, shoulder and back pain.

Marks	Criteria
2	• Detailed list of risks associated with long periods of sitting
1	• Mentions at least one relevant point

8. More natural light can be achieved by:
   - Adding mirrors to reflect light
   - Install transparent or semi-transparent partitions instead of solid ones
   - Replace solid doors with glass doors
   - Reposition book cases and filing cabinets so they don't obstruct light coming in windows

Marks	Criteria
2	• Mentions a range of things that can be done to increase natural light
1	• Mentions at least one relevant point

9. Some changes at little or no cost could include introducing a lunchtime challenge, making a rule that no-one is allowed to eat lunch at their desk or allowing pets at work one day a week.

Marks	Criteria
2	• Mentions more than change that cost little or nothing to introduce
1	• Mentions at least one relevant point

10. Records should be kept for budgeting purposes, so progress can be reported to management, to keep everyone informed, to maintain momentum of the program and to assist further planning.

Marks	Criteria
2	• Mentions a number of reasons why records should be kept
1	• Mentions at least one relevant point

11. Action plan is a plan of activities and task responsibilities and a promotional plan is how each activity is going to be promoted and who is responsible for it.

Marks	Criteria
2	• Good explanation of action plans and promotional plans
1	• Mentions at least one relevant point

Multiple choice and true/false:

1	2	3	4	5	6	7	8	9	10
a	b	d	a	b	c	c	b	d	c
11	**12**	**13**	**14**	**15**	**16**	**17**	**18**	**19**	**20**
d	T	T	F	T	F	F	F	T	T
21	**22**	**23**	**24**	**25**	**26**	**27**	**28**	**29**	**30**
F	F	F	T	T	T	T	F	F	T
31	**32**	**33**	**34**	**35**					
T	F	T	F	T					

Extended response:

Answer could include a description of a range of the following strategies and the benefits that are derived from each one:

- Providing flexible working arrangements
- Providing both open plan and closed working environments
- Encouraging open communication
- Recognising and rewarding staff for good work
- Supporting exercise and fitness
- Using sit/stand desks
- Encouraging walking meetings
- Allowing pets in the workplace
- Renovating the office to bring in more natural light
- Providing a lunchroom
- Providing a free fruit bowl
- Starting up a work sport team
- Sending staff on a team bonding day

Marks	Criteria
13-15	• Demonstrates an extensive knowledge and understanding of strategies that can improve workplace wellbeing • Clearly explains the relationship between new strategies and the subsequent improvement in workplace wellbeing • Communicates ideas and information using relevant workplace examples and industry terminology • Presents a logical and cohesive response
10-12	• Demonstrates a sound knowledge and understanding of strategies that can improve workplace wellbeing • Explains the relationship between new strategies and the subsequent improvement in workplace wellbeing • Communicates using relevant workplace examples and industry terminology • Presents a logical response
7-9	• Demonstrates some knowledge and understanding of strategies that can improve workplace wellbeing • Shows some relationship between new strategies and the subsequent improvement in workplace wellbeing • Communicates using some workplace examples and industry terminology • Demonstrates some organisation in presenting information
4-6	• Demonstrates basic knowledge and/or understanding of workplace wellbeing • Uses some industry terminology
1-3	• Provides some relevant information

Chapter 5:

Note: These tasks are not awarded marks. Submitted answers will be marked as competent or not yet competent. Any task that is deemed not yet competent must be reviewed, updated and resubmitted until it has been deemed competent. Record the date when deemed competent.

Task	Competent	Not yet competent
Task 1: part a.		
Task 1: part b.		
Task 2		
Task 3		
Task 4		
Task 5: part a.		
Task 5: part b.		
Task 6		

Notes

_____

_____

_____

_____

_____

_____

_____

_____

_____

_____

_____

_____

_____

_____

_____

_____

_____

_____

_____

_____

_____

_____

_____

_____

_____

_____

_____

_____

_____

_____

_____

_____

Contents

Glossary of key terms for assessment

Using the glossary will help students to understand what is expected in responses in examinations and assessment tasks.

Account: Account for: state reasons for, report on. Give an account of: narrate a series of events or transactions

Analyse: Identify components and the relationship between them; draw out and relate implications

Apply: Use, utilise, employ in a particular situation

Appreciate: Make a judgement about the value of

Assess: Make a judgement of value, quality, outcomes, results or size

Calculate: Ascertain/determine from given facts, figures or information

Clarify: Make clear or plain

Classify: Arrange or include in classes/categories

Compare: Show how things are similar or different

Construct: Make; build; put together items or arguments

Contrast: Show how things are different or opposite

Critically: (analyse/ evaluate)   Add a degree or level of accuracy depth, knowledge and understanding, logic, questioning, reflection and quality to (analyse/evaluate)

Deduce: Draw conclusions

Define: State meaning and identify essential qualities

Demonstrate: Show by example

Describe: Provide characteristics and features

Discuss: Identify issues and provide points for and/or against

Distinguish: Recognise or note/indicate as being distinct or different from; to note differences between

Evaluate: Make a judgement based on criteria; determine the value of

Examine:	Inquire into
Explain:	Relate cause and effect; make the relationships between things evident; provide why and/or how
Extract:	Choose relevant and/or appropriate details
Extrapolate:	Infer from what is known
Identify:	Recognise and name
Interpret:	Draw meaning from
Investigate:	Plan, inquire into and draw conclusions about
Justify:	Support an argument or conclusion
Outline:	Sketch in general terms; indicate the main features of
Predict:	Suggest what may happen based on available information
Propose:	Put forward (for example a point of view, idea, argument, suggestion) for consideration or action
Recall:	Present remembered ideas, facts or experiences
Recommend:	Provide reasons in favour
Recount:	Retell a series of events
Summarise:	Express, concisely, the relevant details
Synthesise:	Putting together various elements to make a whole

Chapter 1: Select and prepare to use technology

Short answer:

1. What should be taken into consideration before preparing a document or presentation?

    (2 marks)

    _____

    _____

    _____

2. What questions do you ask to determine the type of document that best suits the needs of the audience?

    (4 marks)

    _____

    _____

    _____

    _____

3. What information should be included about the business on all documents?   (2 marks)

    _____

    _____

4. What is the main advantage of using the style function when creating a document? (1 mark)

    _____

    _____

5. Why is it important to set up a computer station correctly?

    (2 marks)

    _____

    _____

    _____

6. How high should a desk be?

    (1 mark)

    _____

    _____

7. When should a footrest be used? (2 marks)

_____

_____

_____

8. If you have to use two computer screens, how should they be positioned? (2 marks)

_____

_____

_____

_____

9. Why is it important to stand on an anti-fatigue mat at a standing desk? (1 mark)

_____

10. Where should a desk be positioned in relation to overhead lights? (1 mark)

_____

11. List what you can do to reduce fatigue and repetitive injuries if you work at a desk all day.

(3 marks)

_____

_____

_____

_____

_____

_____

_____

12. How can noise be reduced in an open-plan office? (2 marks)

_____

_____

_____

_____

13. What is the ideal temperature for air conditioning in an office?   (2 marks)

_____

_____

_____

Multiple choice:

1. What determines how much technical information should be included in a document?
    a. How it must be formatted
    b. The level of knowledge of the audience
    c. If it must follow organisational guidelines
    d. Whether the document is for an internal or external client

2. What software would be used for spreadsheets?
    a. Skype
    b. QuickBooks
    c. Office Suite
    d. Microsoft Edge

3. Why should desks be adjusted ergonomically?
    a. So the desk looks good
    b. To alleviate neck and back pain
    c. So many people can use the same desk
    d. To allow the chair to fit properly under the desk

4. What should you do if a chair is too low for the desk?
    a. Raise the desk height
    b. Find a higher chair to use
    c. Place blocks under the chair legs
    d. Raise the chair and use a footrest

5. Why should a document holder be in line with the computer monitor?
    a. It can be reached
    b. It can be seen easily
    c. It looks neat and tidy
    d. It is parallel to the edge of the desk

6. When should a monitor be placed slightly towards one side?
    a. To avoid eye strain
    b. To reduce glare and shadows on the screen
    c. When using two monitors for unequal amounts of time
    d. So it looks like you are using two monitors and are always busy

7. How can you reduce fatigue when using a computer all day?
    a. Use a sit/stand desk
    b. Reduce glare coming from windows
    c. Place noisy machines in a different room
    d. Adjust the air conditioning so it isn't too hot

8. What can cause headaches and eye strain?
    a. Glare coming from a window
    b. Noise coming from a photocopier
    c. Not aligning computer screen correctly
    d. Being positioned too close to the lunch room

9. In what type of environment do workers experience more problems?
    a. Offices without carpet on the floor
    b. Open plan offices without partitions
    c. Small rooms without proper storage
    d. Offices with photocopier in the middle of the room

10. At what temperature should an air conditioner be set?
    a. Between 20 and 24 degrees in summer and one degree lower in winter
    b. Between 22 and 25 degrees in summer and one degree lower in winter
    c. Between 21 and 24 degrees in summer and two degrees lower in winter
    d. Between 21 and 25 degrees in summer and two degrees lower in winter

True or false?

11. A business logo must be included in all documents at the top of every page.

12. The file name, author and page number should be included in the header.

13. Most documents are printed on A4 paper.

14. The more complex a document, the more planning should go into it before it is created.

15. Formatting can apply the same font to the entire document.

16. Invoices are generated from spreadsheets.

17. A chair used for computer work should support the curve of your spine.

18. There should be a gap of 75mm between your knees and your chair.

19. The top of the computer monitor should be parallel to your eye level.

20. The monitor should be tilted slightly forward if using a standing desk.

21. Bright light should come from above the computer rather than from the side.

22. In order to reduce fatigue, you should change your posture many times during the day.

23. Improper lighting can cause headaches and eyestrain.

24. Fluorescent lights can help to reduce glare on computer screens.

25. Every two desks should have a photocopier to share.

26. Non-reflective desk surfaces can help to reduce reflection.

27. Noise from photocopiers can increase stress levels.

28. Carpet on the floor can help to absorb noise.

29. Airconditioning vents should be close to workers to keep them cool in summer.

30. Open plan offices are good for privacy if the desks aren't too close to each other.

Write clues for the following completed crossword:

Across:

2. _____

_____

8. _____

_____

11. _____

_____

12. _____

_____

14. _____

_____

16. _____

_____

17. _____

_____

18. _____

_____

19. _____

_____

20. _____

_____

Down:

1. _____

_____

3. _____

_____

4. _____

_____

5. _____

_____

6. _____

_____

7. _____

_____

9. _____

_____

18. _____

_____

19. _____

_____

20. _____

_____

Crossword:

Across:

2. When using a standing desk, how should the monitor be positioned? (2 words)

4. Page orientation used for wide tables.

7. This can be pre-set when creating a new document. (2 words)

8. This should be placed directly in front of you on a desk.

11. These should fit comfortably under a desk.

13. These needs must be considered when setting up a workstation.

14. Where photocopiers should be located. (2 words)

16. These types of documents require more planning.

17. These must be included on every letter. (2 words)

18. These can be formatted to look the same.

20. Level of this will determine how much explanation needs to be included in business correspondence.

Down:

1. What is generally outlined in storage protocols for documents? (2 words)

3. These help to absorb noise in an open plan office.

5. These can be caused by loud equipment in an office.

6. This is done to make a document consistent.

9. This can be reduced by partially closing blinds.

10. Another name for typing a document. (2 words)

12. These can be caused by poor air quality.

15. This is important for comfort on chairs.

19. This must be within easy reach.

Extended response 1:

a) How do you determine what software to use to produce a document or presentation?

(3 marks)

_____

_____

_____

_____

_____

_____

b) Explain what protocols a business might have regarding document creation. (3 marks)

_____

_____

_____

_____

_____

_____

_____

_____

_____

_____

_____

_____

_____

c) Explain how you would adjust your workspace, furniture and equipment to suit your own ergonomic requirements. (9 marks)

_____

_____

_____

_____

_____

_____

Extended response 2:

Explain the relationship between ergonomics and health and safety within the business services industry.

(15 marks)

Your answer will be assessed on how well you:
- demonstrate knowledge and understanding relevant to the question
- communicate ideas and information using relevant workplace examples and industry terminology
- present a logical and cohesive response

_____

_____

_____

_____

_____

_____

_____

_____

_____

_____

_____

_____

_____

_____

_____

_____

_____

_____

_____

_____

_____

_____

_____

Chapter 2: Input and process information or data

Short answer:

1. What software program would you use for each of the following: (6 marks)

    a.   Text documents: _____

    b.   Databases: _____

    c.   Electronic slide shows: _____

    d.   Emails: _____

    e.   Spreadsheets: _____

    f.   Note-taking: _____

2. What can be produced using Microsoft Word?   (2 marks)

_____

_____

_____

_____

3. Why are spreadsheets an essential business tool?   (2 marks)

_____

_____

_____

_____

4. Identify advantages of using PowerPoint.   (2 marks)

_____

_____

_____

_____

5. What types of information can be stored in a database? (2 marks)

_____

_____

_____

6. Identify specific requirements a business may have regarding the entry of information. (4 marks)

_____

_____

_____

_____

7. In a spreadsheet, what is a cell? (2 marks)

_____

_____

_____

8. How is a cell in a spreadsheet identified? (1 mark)

_____

9. What is a value in a spreadsheet? (1 mark)

_____

10. How are text and values aligned in a spreadsheet? (2 marks)

_____

11. How can a cell be formatted? (3 marks)

_____

_____

_____

12. Why don't you use currency symbols in a spreadsheet? (1 mark)

_____

13. What is important so a document is an effective way of communication? (3 marks)

_____

_____

_____

_____

14. What business information has to be regularly updated? (2 marks)

_____

_____

_____

_____

15. What are the four most common types of formatting used in word processing? (3 marks)

_____

_____

_____

_____

_____

_____

16. When can you use colour in a spreadsheet? (2 marks)

_____

_____

_____

17. What is a specific application function in Microsoft Excel? (1 mark)

_____

18. Why is using a function more accurate than using a formula in spreadsheets? (1 mark)

_____

19. What does the F1 key do in Microsoft Word? (1 mark)

_____

Multiple choice:

1. What program is most suitable for creating business cards?
   a. Access
   b. Excel
   c. OneNote
   d. Publisher

2. What program can be used for financial analysis?
   a. Access
   b. Excel
   c. OneNote
   d. Word

3. What is a hyperlink?
   a. Super text
   b. Data reference
   c. Hyphenated words
   d. Leads to another document

4. What is the primary purpose of a spreadsheet?
   a. To generate charts to make comparisons easier
   b. To organise and categorise data in a logical form
   c. To make sure that money is not being misappropriated
   d. To save a lot of time due to automatic arithmetic functions

5. What program allows videos to be included?
   a. Excel
   b. OneNote
   c. PowerPoint
   d. Word

6. What is an organisational requirement for entering data?
   a. Writing styles
   b. Confidentiality
   c. Performance plans
   d. Quality assessments

7. What document strives for consistency and quality in documents produced?
   a. Style guide
   b. Graphics manual
   c. Communications manual
   d. Writing policy and procedure

8. What types of data can be entered into a spreadsheet?
    a. Dates, names and labels
    b. Text, names and numbers
    c. Labels, values and formulas
    d. Numbers, dates and formulas

9. Why is there generally a limit of one table per spreadsheet worksheet?
    a. Styling is easier
    b. One type of data can be entered
    c. Information doesn't get confusing
    d. Easier to keep the formatting the same

10. What is checked during proofreading?
    a. File name is correct
    b. Accuracy and consistency
    c. Columns are the correct size
    d. Information has been updated

11. In a spreadsheet, what is generally found in the second row?
    a. The author
    b. Row headings
    c. Column headings
    d. The name of the spreadsheet

12. What alignment is used in a spreadsheet?
    a. Everything is aligned left
    b. Everything is aligned right
    c. Values aligned left and text aligned right
    d. Text aligned left and values aligned right

13. How can headings be highlighted?
    a. Use bold and italics
    b. Use bold and colour
    c. Use italics and colour
    d. Use italics and capital letters

True or false?

14. OneNote is an information management tool.

15. Microsoft Word can be used in different operating systems.

16. Formatting tools can change and control the appearance of documents.

17. Spreadsheets can track business income and expenditure.

18. Charts and not graphs can be generated in Excel.

19. PowerPoint presentations can be saved as a web page.

20. The software chosen will depend on the type and amount of information to be entered.

21. Organisational requirements include presentation assurance.

22. Naming conventions and filing protocols go hand-in-hand.

23. Spreadsheets are divided into rows and columns.

24. A cell in a spreadsheet is labelled by the row number then the column number.

25. Text wrap can be used to limit the text displayed in a cell.

26. 12-Dec is a short date compared to 12/12/2021.

27. Information and data should be checked and amended when necessary.

28. Accurate information can cause problems and confusion if not amended.

29. Character formatting determines how text appears on the page.

30. Page formatting includes alignment of columns.

31. Arial 11 is the default font in Excel.

32. Adjusting the column width and height gives the data room.

33. Solid lines can be used for column borders.

34. Formatting tools are located at the top of the screen.

35. =MAX(D2:D8) is the function to find the maximum value in the cells D2 and D8.

Write clues for the following completed crossword:

The crossword contains the following answers:

- 1 Down: PUBLISHER
- 2 Down: PRESET
- 3 Down: SUBDIVISION
- 4 Across: DEFAULT FORMAT
- 5 Down: MICROSOFT
- 6 Across: WHOLE VALUE
- 7 Down: ETHICAL BEHAVIOR
- 8 Down: GRAPHS AND CHARTS
- 9 Across: NAMING CONVENTIONS
- 10 Down: MEDIA
- 11 Across: WRAP TEXT
- 12 Across: INDENTATION
- 13 Down: LOGICAL FORMA
- 14 Across: PROBLEMS
- 15 Across: DECIMAL POINTS
- 16 Across: CONFUSION
- 17 Across: CAPITALS
- 18 Down: CONSISTENCY
- 19 Across: PROCEDURES MANUAL
- 20 Across: HORIZONTAL

Across:

4. _____

_____

6. _____

_____

9. _____

_____

11. _____

12. _____
_____

14. _____
_____

15. _____
_____

16. _____
_____

17. _____
_____

19. _____
_____

20. _____
_____

Down:

1. _____
_____

2. _____
_____

3. _____
_____

5. _____
_____

7. _____
_____

8. _____
_____

10. _____
_____

13. _____
_____

18. _____

_____

Crossword:

Across:

4. Spreadsheets are often used for these.

6. When a presentation is done on the web using Zoom.

8. Found in spreadsheets.

9. These surround arguments in application functions.

12. This must be done to information in order to keep it up to date.

13. These are located at the top of the spreadsheet.

14. Documents should be saved regularly to prevent this from happening.

16. These can be added to a PowerPoint presentation.

17. A whole value does not have this.

18. This is generally found in the first column of a spreadsheet.

19. What has the magnifying glass symbol in it?

20. It is important that this is always correct in every business document.

Down:

1. These should not be dark in a spreadsheet.

2. These are pre-set formulas that can be used in a spreadsheet.

3. Systems and processes are looked at under this requirement.

5. This can be created in a Word document.

7. Used for sending and receiving emails.

10. This can be affected if the business does not have professional-looking documentation.

11. Program used for storing customer data.

15. Data can be sorted this way.

Extended response 1:

a) Why are organisational requirements for the input of data important? Include examples.

(4 marks)

_____

_____

_____

_____

_____

_____

_____

_____

b) How is consistency and quality in documentation achieved?   (4 marks)

_____

_____

_____

_____

_____

_____

_____

_____

c) Explain how formatting improves the appearance of a document.   (7 marks)

_____

_____

_____

_____

_____

_____

_____

_____

Extended response 2:

Explain how organisational requirements affect the processing of information or data in documents. Include examples. (15 marks)

Your answer will be assessed on how well you:
- demonstrate knowledge and understanding relevant to the question
- communicate ideas and information using relevant workplace examples and industry terminology
- present a logical and cohesive response

_____

_____

_____

_____

_____

_____

_____

_____

_____

_____

_____

_____

_____

_____

_____

_____

_____

_____

_____

_____

_____

_____

Chapter 3: Finalise and store document

Short answer:

1. What is checked in a document to ensure its accuracy? (2 marks)

   _____

   _____

2. Why shouldn't you just rely on the auto spell check when checking spelling? (2 marks)

   _____

3. Why should you review the format of the whole document? (2 marks)

   _____

4. Why is it important that the information in a document is factual? (1 mark)

   _____

5. What is metadata in a spreadsheet? (2 marks)

   _____

   _____

   _____

6. How do you remove metadata? (2 marks)

   _____

   _____

   _____

   _____

   _____

7. What is a file? (2 marks)

   _____

   _____

   _____

8. How are files stored? (2 marks)

   _____

9. What should be recorded on the front of a paper-based file? (2 marks)

_____

_____

_____

10. List how electronic files can be stored on a computer system. (3 marks)

_____

_____

11. Under what topics can folders be filed? (2 marks)

_____

_____

12. What is a File Naming Convention? (2 marks)

_____

_____

_____

13. What is a revision numbering system? (2 marks)

_____

_____

_____

_____

14. When should "copy" be included in a file name? (2 marks)

_____

_____

_____

15. What should you do when you start a new document? (1 mark)

_____

16. Why is it important to save a document every few minutes? (1 mark)

_____

Multiple choice:

1. For what should all documents be checked?
    a. Sentences should match the purpose of the document
    b. Sentences should be long with a lot of technical information
    c. Sentences should not be too long and be written with appropriate tone
    d. Sentences should be formatted so mistakes show accuracy of the facts

2. What is metadata?
    a. Large sized font
    b. Identifying information
    c. Large amounts of data
    d. Another name for megadata

3. What is a file?
    a. A folder on a computer
    b. A suspension folder in a filing cabinet
    c. Unit of documents on the same subject
    d. Pares that are kept for five years then recycled

4. What is NOT on the cover of a file?
    a. Title
    b. Date opened
    c. File attachments
    d. Reference number

5. Hyphenated names should be treated as one name in what type of filing classification?
    a. Alphabetical
    b. Chronological
    c. Geographical
    d. Subject matter

6. What filing classification is often used in conjunction with other filing methods?
    a. Alphabetical
    b. Chronological
    c. Geographical
    d. Subject matter

7. Where are most electronic files stored?
    a. In an external hard drive
    b. In folders in Microsoft Word
    c. On a file server in one location
    d. In a root folder like My Documents

8. How should dates be recorded in file names so that they display chronologically?
    a. DD-MM-YY
    b. YY-MM-DD
    c. DD-MM-YYYY
    d. YYYY-MM-DD

9. Why are abbreviations used in file names?
    a. To keep the language common for all files
    b. So the length of the file name is not too long
    c. To keep symbols, hyphens and spaces to a minimum
    d. So workers full names are not displayed for anonymity

10. What is important when documents are saved on a network?
    a. Only one person should access the files at any one time
    b. No document should be downloaded onto a personal computer
    c. An open file should be read and amended quickly then saved and closed
    d. The word "copy" is included in the file name if someone has run off a copy

True or false?

11. The purpose of a document should match the tone and style.

12. Margins, alignment and justification should all be consistent throughout a document.

13. Logo should always be positioned in the middle of the top of the page.

14. Factual information is essential for the reputation of the business.

15. Metadata cannot be removed from a spreadsheet.

16. Businesses today have either a paper-based or electronic filing system.

17. Before creating a new file, check that one doesn't already exist with the name you want to use.

18. The name of the person responsible for the file should be recorded on the front cover.

19. Files should go form the oldest at the front to the newest at the back.

20. Never file duplicate files.

21. File attachments, enclosures or supporting documents attached to the documents to which they pertain

22. Bulky items should be placed in an envelope before filing.

23. Copies of documents should be labelled as copies.

24. Numerical files should be cross-referenced to a geographical file.

25. When filing by subject area, files should also be files alpha-numerically.

26. When filed documents have to be accessed by more than one person, they should be stored on a file server.

27. Every business has its own system of naming and storing files.

28. Folders should be named according to the area of work they relate to.

29. A File Naming Convention is used when a large number of documents have to be filed at the one time.

30. No more than three numbers should be used in the name of a file.

31. Another number is always added when a file is amended.

32. v03_01 means a minor change has been made to the third version of a document.

33. When a document has been finished with, it should be marked as "final".

34. Little work will be lost in a power failure if it has been saved regularly.

35. All saved documents should be closed for security reasons.

Write clues for the following completed crossword:

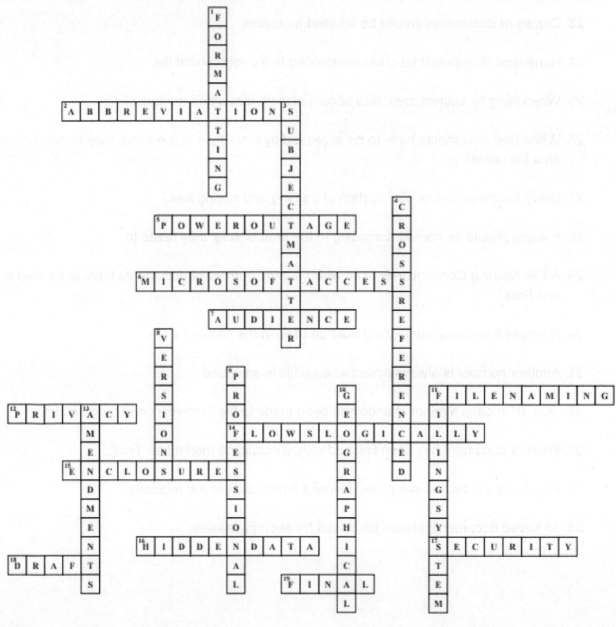

The completed crossword contains the following answers:

1. Down: FORMATTING
2. Across: ABBREVIATION
3. Down: SUBJECTMATTER
4. Down: CROSSREFERENCE
5. Across: POWEROUTAGE
6. Across: MICROSOFTACCESS
7. Across: AUDIENCE
8. Down: VERSION
9. Down: PROFESSIONAL
10. Down: GENERIC
11. Across: FILENAMING / Down: FILINGSYSTEM
12. Across: PRIVACY
13. Down: AMENDMENTS
14. Across: FLOWSLOGICALLY
15. Across: ENCLOSURES
16. Across: HIDDENDATA
17. Across: SECURITY
18. Across: DRAFT
19. Across: FINAL

Across:

2. _____

_____

5. _____

_____

6. _____

_____

7. _____

_____

11. _____

_____

12. _____

_____

14. _____

_____

15. _____

_____

16. _____

_____

17. _____

_____

18. _____

_____

19. _____

_____

Down:

1. _____

_____

3. _____

_____

4. _____

_____

8. _____

_____

9. _____

_____

10. _____

_____

11. _____

_____

13. _____

_____

Crossword:

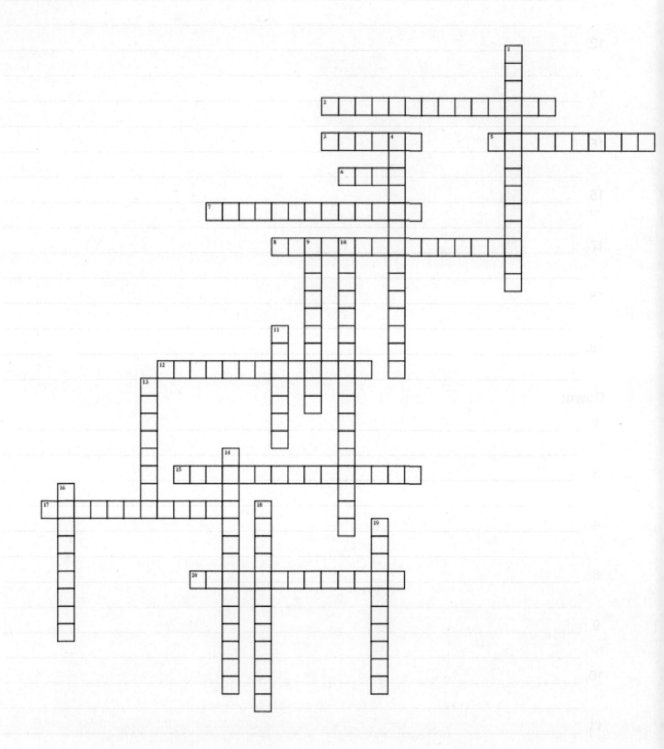

Across:

2. This should be done when a new document has been finished. (3 words)

3. These should be placed in a position that doesn't overwhelm the text in a document.

5. Where documents are stored on a desktop computer. (2 words)

6. This button should be pressed every few minutes when creating a document.

7. Classification of files where records are sorted according to the date.

8. This should be included on the front of every folder of documents. (2 words)

12. These are needed to keep the length of a file name from becoming too long.

15. Reason why files are not destroyed when finished with. (2 words)

17. This should be included at the top of a business letter. (2 words)

20. Where paper copies of documents are filed. (2 words)

Down:

1. A table that notes changes made in documents. (2 words)

4. Folders of documents should be arranged in this way.

9. Describes what a file contains and how they relate to other files. (2 words)

10. Indicates when changes have been made to a file. (2 words)

11. It is very important that this is checked for accuracy.

13. The format of these should be consistent throughout a document.

14. Be wary using this. (3 words)

16. Type of filing system from low to high.

18. This can be a part of metadata. (2 words)

19. Most businesses still use this type of filing system. (2 words)

Extended response 1:

a) Explain the process of proofreading a document. (4 marks)

_____

_____

_____

_____

_____

_____

_____

_____

b) Explain why and how metadata should be removed from a spreadsheet. (4 marks)

_____

_____

_____

_____

_____

_____

_____

_____

_____

c) Explain how documents are named and filed. (7 marks)

_____

_____

_____

_____

_____

_____

Extended response 2:

Explain how final information or data is reviewed and prepared for storage in accordance with organisational and task requirements. (15 marks)

Your answer will be assessed on how well you:
- demonstrate knowledge and understanding relevant to the question
- communicate ideas and information using relevant workplace examples and industry terminology
- present a logical and cohesive response

_____

_____

_____

_____

_____

_____

_____

_____

_____

_____

_____

_____

_____

_____

_____

_____

_____

_____

_____

_____

_____

_____

_____

Chapter 4: Assessment tasks to provide evidence of ability and demonstration of knowledge of topic

Each student must provide evidence of the ability to:

- **select and use at least three business software applications on two occasions each**
- **select and use technology safely and according to organisational requirements**
- **identify and address faults according to requirements**

Instructions:

Each student is to complete their own answers for this section. Submitted answers will be marked as competent or not yet competent. Any task that is deemed not yet competent must be reviewed, updated and resubmitted until it has been deemed competent.

All work must be saved in a folder named "Northern Beaches Bike Tours", using the headings "Exercise 1", "Exercise 2" etc. A printed copy of each exercise must be handed in for marking in a portfolio, making sure that each exercise is clearly labelled and in the correct order.

Simulation Exercise – Northern Beaches Bike Tours

Congratulations and welcome to Northern Beaches Bike Tours. You have been hired as a computer specialist because of your skills using many different kinds of software applications. We hope you find your work here both challenging and exciting.

We are a relatively new business, operating for just over a year. We rent out bicycles for the day and provide motorbike tours along the Northern Beaches. Most of our customers are tourists from overseas.

Exercise 1:

Design a new logo for the business using Microsoft Word. It should include the business name and should not be any larger than 3cm by 5cm. Save it as a BMP and a JPG file. Print a copy for your portfolio.

Note: go to the following website for information on how to create a business logo using Microsoft Word.
https://www.logaster.com/blog/how-to-create-awesome-logo-easily-with-microsoft-word/

Exercise 2:

Create a new letterhead for Northern Beaches Bike Tours. The letterhead should include the business name, address, phone number and the logo created in Exercise 1.

Address: 2552 Collaroy Beach Road, Collaroy Beach 2098
Phone: use your own phone number

Instructions:

1. Use a decorative font for the name in size 18-24 points. Include the logo you have designed. Add a horizontal line to separate the letterhead from the rest of the letter. Proofread, save, print a copy and place it in your portfolio.

2. Go to "Help" and find out how to save this letterhead as a template. Print a copy of these instructions and place it in your portfolio. Save the letterhead as a template.

Exercise 3:

Northern Beaches Bike Tours uses memorandums to communicate within the business. Use the information below to write the memo in your own words as if it came from the owner of the business. Proofread, save and print a copy for your portfolio.

From: Alan Smith
To: All employees
Date: (use today's date)

1st paragraph: Write telling the employees that this is a new price list for the coming summer.

2nd paragraph: Make a 4-column table using the following price information. (The " | " tells where the columns are). Note: one day is from 9am until 4pm.

Tour | Length | Amenities | Cost

Bike | 1 day | bike rental | $50

Easy ride | 1 day | bike rental, BBQ lunch, guide | $100

Scenic | 1 day | bike rental, gourmet picnic lunch, guide | $120

Bike 'n fish | 1 day | bike rental, fishing gear, BBQ lunch, guide | $120

Beach bash | 2 hours | motor bike rental and driver | $150

Super beach bash | 3 hours | motor bike rental, driver, gourmet lunch | $250

3rd paragraph: Tell the employees that you are looking forward to a great summer. Then thank them for the good work they have been doing.

Exercise 4:

Design a new business card for yourself. On the business card include the business name, address, phone number, your name and the business logo that you have already designed. Proofread, save and print a page of at least 6 business cards for your portfolio.

Exercise 5:

Write a promotional letter to send to many of the local businesses asking them if they would like to be a sponsor for the up-coming Australia Day Bike Ride and BBQ. Create a database using the names and addresses of 10 local businesses you could approach for such sponsorship. Save this database using an appropriate name. Using mail merge, write a letter on your business letterhead to send to each of these businesses. Proofread, save and print a copy for your portfolio.

Information for letter:

1st paragraph: Tell them that we appreciated their support for last year's event and for letting us place our pamphlets at their place of work.

2nd paragraph: Ask them to include our Australia Day Bike Ride and BBQ on their calendar of events. Ask them if they would be willing to support the event with a $1000 sponsorship donation. In return, we will put their logo on our flyers and T-shirts for the event. Ask them to contact us by next Friday. (use next Friday's date)

Last paragraph: Thank them for their support. Tell them we are looking forward to hearing from them and working with them.

Closing: Yours faithfully, and type the signature of the owner, leaving room for your signature.

Exercise 6:

Create an A4-sized flyer that can be put in the local newspaper and can be mailed out with the promotional letters. The flyer will include a border, the title, a graphic or logo and the details of the event above. Make sure you include the business name, address and phone number.

Details: Meet in the car park behind the Collaroy Surf Life Saving Club at 10am; ride to Newport Beach for a great BBQ (everything provided); cost is $50 for adults, $25 for kids under 18, free for kids under 5; free t-shirts for all registered participants; bring the whole family; register now.

Instructions: add your name in small font in the bottom right corner of the footer; preview your flyer for balance and layout on the page, making any adjustments to create a well-balanced flyer; proofread, save and print a copy for your portfolio.

Exercise 7:

Make a folding card that can be used as a special invitation for the Australia Day Bike Ride and BBQ.

Information:

Front: Border, the name of the event and a related graphic.

Back: Northern Beaches Bike Tours, the business logo, created by ......(your name) and 20XX copyright.

Inside: You are invited to attend .... (use the details in Exercise 6 above)

Instructions: Make sure you choose a folding card in the appropriate desktop publishing software. Use a decorative font for the title. Preview your card and make any adjustments necessary to create a well-designed card. Proofread, save and print a copy for your portfolio.

Exercise 8:

Create a spreadsheet to show the monthly and projected yearly budgets, using the following information. Use the correct formulas to work out the totals.

Information:

Account	Monthly	Yearly
Income		
Tours	25600	?
Rentals	4500	?
	----------	----------
Total income	?	?
Expenses:		
Rent	1200	?
Wages	16000	?
Bike Repairs	400	?
Advertising	250	?
Utilities	325	?
Insurance	250	?
	----------	----------
Total Expenses	?	?
	----------	----------
Net Income	?	?

Instructions:

1. Open Microsoft Excel

2. Enter the title Northern Beaches Bike Tours and bold it, using Arial font size 18.

3. Add "prepared by …….. (your name)" and make it italics, using font size 12.

4. Enter the data above using Arial font, size 11.

5. Calculate the yearly amounts by multiplying the monthly amounts by 12 (using the correct cell numbers)

6. Use the SUM function to total the Income and Expenses.

7. Calculate the Net Income by using the formula =Total Income – Total Expenses (using the correct cell numbers)

8. Use whole numbers, no decimal places.

9. Format the bottom row of numbers to currency and no decimal places.

10. Adjust column widths as needed so they are spaced evenly.

11. Align column headings.

12. Adjust margins.

13. Preview, proofread, save (as NBBTbudget) and print a copy for your portfolio.

14. Close the program.

Exercise 9:

Your job includes preparing the yearly budget for which you need to make some projections.

Instructions:

1. Open Microsoft Excel.

2. Open your NBBTbudget spreadsheet.

3. Change the title to "Forecast Budget for Northern Beaches Bike Tours".

4. Make the following changes to the monthly figures:

   a. Rentals income to 5500

   b. Tours Income to 28600

   c. Advertising to 750

   d. Wages to 18000

   e. Insurance to 350

5. Save as NBBTbudget2

6. Preview, proofread and print a copy for your portfolio.

Exercise 10:

We need you to create a database of our customers. Fill in the following registration cards using your classmates' information.

Northern Beaches Bike Tours	Northern Beaches Bike Tours
Registration Card	**Registration Card**
Name:	**Name:**
Address:	**Address:**

```
┌─────────────────────────────────┐   ┌─────────────────────────────────┐
│   Northern Beaches Bike Tours   │   │   Northern Beaches Bike Tours   │
│                                 │   │                                 │
│   Registration Card             │   │   Registration Card             │
│                                 │   │                                 │
│                                 │   │                                 │
│   Name:                         │   │   Name:                         │
│                                 │   │                                 │
│   Address:                      │   │   Address:                      │
│                                 │   │                                 │
└─────────────────────────────────┘   └─────────────────────────────────┘

    ┌─────────────────────────────────┐   ┌─────────────────────────────────┐
    │   Northern Beaches Bike Tours   │   │   Northern Beaches Bike Tours   │
    │                                 │   │                                 │
    │   Registration Card             │   │   Registration Card             │
    │                                 │   │                                 │
    │                                 │   │                                 │
    │   Name:                         │   │   Name:                         │
    │                                 │   │                                 │
    │   Address:                      │   │   Address:                      │
    │                                 │   │                                 │
    └─────────────────────────────────┘   └─────────────────────────────────┘
```

Instructions:

1. Open the appropriate software program.
2. Use the following fields: surname, first name, address, suburb, state, post code
3. Enter the data you have written down above.
4. Proofread, save and print it in table form.
5. Sort the database by surname and print it in table form.
6. Add two more customers:

```
┌─────────────────────────────────┐   ┌─────────────────────────────────┐
│   Northern Beaches Bike Tours   │   │   Northern Beaches Bike Tours   │
│                                 │   │                                 │
│   Registration Card             │   │   Registration Card             │
│                                 │   │                                 │
│                                 │   │                                 │
│   Name:                         │   │   Name:                         │
│                                 │   │                                 │
│   Address:                      │   │   Address:                      │
│                                 │   │                                 │
└─────────────────────────────────┘   └─────────────────────────────────┘
```

7. Create a report called "Customer Address Report" with a subtitle "prepared by ……. (your name)"

8. Centre and bold the title. Centre and italicise the sub title.

9. Sort the report by the surnames.

10. Proofread, save and print a copy for your portfolio.

Exercise 11:

Create labels for the envelopes for all the customers in our database.

Information: Format the labels for Avery labels. Use the following format:

> First name   Last name
>
> Address
>
> City   State   Postcode

Instructions:

1. Load the customer database

2. Use the software's label feature to create the labels.

3. Use Arial 12-point font.

4. Print the labels on A4 paper if you do not have any labels.

5. Preview, proofread, save and print a copy for your portfolio.

Exercise 12:

You have been with Northern Beaches Bike Tours for twelve months now. Write a report evaluating the success of the business. Include an idea for a new event that you would like to introduce within the next twelve months. Save and print a copy for your portfolio.

Exercise 13:

Write a report identifying any faults experienced while completing this task, and describe how they were addressed, according to requirements. Save and print a copy for your portfolio.

Each student must also demonstrate knowledge of:

- **key features of:**
  - **organisation's work health and safety requirements relevant to own role**
  - **organisation's requirements for file naming and storage**
  - **applications used for organising electronic information and data**

Instructions:

Each student is to complete their own answers for this section. Submitted answers will be marked as competent or not yet competent. Any task that is deemed not yet competent must be reviewed, updated and resubmitted until it has been deemed competent.

The following tasks should be completed either during work placement and/or during visits to local businesses. Students should talk to a worker whose primary job involves working with computers in two different businesses.

Task 1:

Name of business 1:
Name of worker interviewed:
Job role:

Name of business 2:
Name of worker interviewed:
Job role:

Answer the following questions for each business:

1. List the organisation's work health and safety requirements that cover this worker's job role.

2. Are there any other concerns this worker has regarding work health and safety for his/her job role? What changes/improvements does this worker consider should be introduced? Substantiate your answer.

3. What are the organisation's requirements for naming and storing files?

4. List the applications used for organising electronic information and data.

Chapter 5: Marking guidelines and suggested answers

Note: no suggested answers are given for the completed crosswords as answers will vary for each student.

Chapter 1:

1) Should take into account the purpose of the document, who is going to be reading it and the most appropriate format that should be used.

Marks	Criteria
2	• Identifies at least two things that should be taken into account
1	• Identifies one thing that should be taken into account

2) Questions that should be asked include:
   - Who is reading this document or viewing this presentation?
   - Is it an internal or external client?
   - Will they understand technical information?
   - How much prior knowledge do they have of the topic?

Marks	Criteria
4	• Identifies four questions
3	• Identifies three questions
2	• Identifies two questions
1	• Identifies one question

3) Every document should include the business name, address, phone number and email address.

Marks	Criteria
2	• Identifies at least two things that should be included on every document
1	• Identifies one thing that should be included on every document

4) The main advantage of using the style function is that the document has consistency without having to manually format everything as you go.

Marks	Criteria
1	• Identifies that the document has consistency without having to continually format

5. It is important to set up a computer station correctly so it suits the individual user, to alleviate neck and back pain as well as sore wrists and fingers.

Marks	Criteria
2	• Identifies at least two reasons why it is important to set up a computer station correctly
1	• Identifies one reason why it is important to set up a computer station correctly

6. A desk should be high enough to fit your knees, thighs and feet under it.

Marks	Criteria
1	• Identifies how high a desk should be

7. A footrest should be used if the chair has to be raised so the user's thighs are parallel to the floor.

Marks	Criteria
2	• Detailed explanation of when a footrest should be used
1	• Mentions one point about footrests

8. If you are using two screens, and use them equally in time, position them close to each other with the centre of the "v" aligned to your nose. If you use one a lot more than the other, place the main screen directly in front of you and the other one slightly to the side.

Marks	Criteria
2	• Detailed explanation of how two computer screens should be positioned
1	• Mentions one point about computer screens

9. It is important to stand on an anti-fatigue mat at a standing desk to reduce stress on the body.

Marks	Criteria
1	• Identifies why it is important to stand on an anti-fatigue mat

10. A desk should be positioned between rows of lights rather than directly underneath a light.

Marks	Criteria
1	• Identifies where a desk should be positioned

a) To reduce fatigue and repetitive injuries, you can:
- Rotate between a variety of work tasks to change your posture throughout the day
- Use opportunities to move between sitting and standing positions at the workstation
- Move your hand off the mouse or keyboard when not in use
- Place the printer, scanner and photocopier away from the workstation
- Use sit/stand desks
- Stand when talking on the phone
- Eat lunch away from your desk and get up and move regularly

Marks	Criteria
3	• Detailed list of how to reduce fatigue and injuries
2	• Lists two or more ways to reduce fatigue and injuries
1	• Lists one way to reduce fatigue and injuries

b) Noise can be reduced in an open-plan office by placing noisy machinery like photocopiers in a separate room, having carpet on the floors and having screens well positioned to absorb noise.

Marks	Criteria
2	• Detailed explanation of how to reduce noise
1	• Mentions one point about noise

c) Air conditioners should operate at a temperature range of 21-24 degrees in summer and about two degrees lower in winter.

Marks	Criteria
2	• Identifies temperatures for air conditioners in summer and winter
1	• Identifies temperatures for air conditioners in summer OR winter

Multiple choice and true/false:

1	2	3	4	5	6	7	8	9	10
b	c	b	d	b	c	a	a	b	c
11	**12**	**13**	**14**	**15**	**16**	**17**	**18**	**19**	**20**
F	F	T	T	T	F	T	F	T	F
21	**22**	**23**	**24**	**25**	**26**	**27**	**28**	**29**	**30**
F	T	T	T	F	T	T	T	F	F

Crossword:

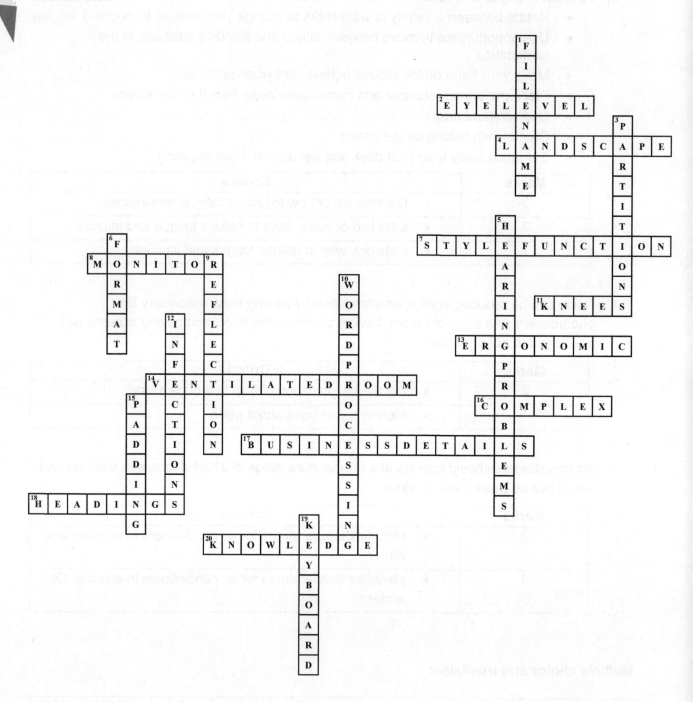

Across:
1. F I L E N A M E (vertical)
2. E Y E L E V E L
4. L A N D S C A P E
3. P A R T I T I O N (vertical)
5. H E A R I N G P R O B L E M S (vertical)
7. S T Y L E F U N C T I O N
6. F O R M A T (vertical)
8. M O N I T O R
9. R E F L E C (vertical)
10. W O R D P R O C E S S I N G (vertical)
11. K N E E S
13. E R G O N O M I C
12. I N F O R M A T I O N (vertical)
14. V E N T I L A T E D R O O M
15. P A D D I N G (vertical)
16. C O M P L E X
17. B U S I N E S S D E T A I L S
18. H E A D I N G S
19. K E Y B O A R D (vertical)
20. K N O W L E D G E

Extended response 1:

a) Answer could include: The software chosen will depend on what type of document or presentation has to be created. This is determined by who will be reading the document or viewing the presentation, if it is an internal or external client, how much technical information they understand and how much prior knowledge they have of the topic.

Marks	Criteria
3	• Demonstrates a sound understanding of computer software and what determines the selection of suitable software to produce a document or presentation
2	• Demonstrates a some understanding of computer software and what determines the selection of suitable software to produce a document or presentation
1	• Provides some relevant information

b) Answer could include: An explanation of the following protocols:
- Inclusion of business details
- Inclusion of business logo
- Size and style of fonts
- Paper sizes
- What to include in headers and footers
- Margin sizes
- Storage of files

Marks	Criteria
3	• Demonstrates a sound understanding of business protocols regarding document creation
2	• Demonstrates a some understanding of business protocols regarding document creation
1	• Provides some relevant information

c) Answer could include: an explanation should be included about the following:
- Height of desk
- Type of chair
- Position of keyboard and mouse
- Position of the monitor
- Position of document holder, telephone and other commonly used objects
- Using two monitors
- Standing desks
- Environmental factors: impact of light, noise and air quality

Marks	Criteria
8-9	• Demonstrates an extensive knowledge of ergonomics when setting up own workspace
6-7	• Demonstrates a thorough knowledge of ergonomics when setting up own workspace
4-5	• Demonstrates some knowledge of ergonomics when setting up own workspace
2-3	• Demonstrates some knowledge of ergonomics
1	• Provides some relevant information

Extended response 2:

Marks	Criteria
13-15	• Demonstrates an extensive knowledge and understanding of ergonomics and health and safety • Clearly explains the relationship between ergonomics and health and safety • Communicates ideas and information using relevant workplace examples and industry terminology • Presents a logical and cohesive response
10-12	• Demonstrates a sound knowledge and understanding of ergonomics and health and safety • Explains the relationship between ergonomics and health and safety • Communicates using relevant workplace examples and industry terminology • Presents a logical response
7-9	• Demonstrates some knowledge and understanding of ergonomics and health and safety • Shows some relationship between ergonomics and health and safety • Communicates using some workplace examples and industry terminology • Demonstrates some organisation in presenting information
4-6	• Demonstrates basic knowledge and/or understanding of ergonomics AND/OR health and safety • Uses some industry terminology
1-3	• Provides some relevant information

Answer could include: To explain the relationship between ergonomics and health and safety, students need to explain the cause and effect of various ergonomic features when setting up a workstation to problems that may affect health and safety of workers. Examples include:

- Chairs: how your spine needs support, personal comfort levels, effect on shoulders
- Keyboard and mouse: wrist pain
- Monitor: eyestrain, neck pain
- Document holders, phones etc: eyestrain, head and neck problems, muscle strain from reaching
- Standing desks: fatigue, back problems
- Light: headaches and eye strain
- Noise: hearing problems, interrupted concentration, stress
- Air quality: headaches, tiredness, irritations of the eyes, nose and throat

Chapter 2:

1) Software programs: 1 mark for each correct answer
   - Word
   - Access
   - PowerPoint
   - Outlook
   - Excel
   - OneNote

2) Microsoft Word can produce many kinds of documents, like letters, reports, calendars, resumes, brochures, appointment schedules, certificates, invoices, business cards, newsletters, agendas, flyers, envelopes, memos, labels, quotes etc.

Marks	Criteria
2	• Identifies many types of documents that Microsoft Word can produce
1	• Identifies one type of document that Microsoft Word can produce

3) Spreadsheets are an essential business tool as they organise and categorise data in a logical format; formulas can be used to make calculations; and they help to identify trends or to make forecasts.

Marks	Criteria
2	• Detailed explanation of why spreadsheets are an essential business tool
1	• Identifies one reason why spreadsheets are an essential business tool

4) Advantages of using PowerPoint include: can be used for presentations for a large group; can be used in "real time" presentations on Zoom etc; allows you to use custom animation; can add photos, videos and sound effects; can embed videos from YouTube; can save the presentation as a webpage; can print presentations as handouts.

Marks	Criteria
2	• Detailed list of advantages of PowerPoint
1	• Identifies one advantage of PowerPoint

5) A database can store customer data (like names, addresses, phone numbers and email addresses), orders placed, product information, supplier information and details about employees.

Marks	Criteria
2	• Identifies many types of information that can be stored in a database
1	• Identifies one type of information that can be stored in a database

6) Specific requirements may include:
   • Spelling, grammar, punctuation and writing style
   • Document naming conventions and filing protocols
   • Visual presentation, including margins, fonts and style
   • Graphics standards, including the use of logos and brands

Marks	Criteria
4	• Identifies four requirements
3	• Identifies three requirements
2	• Identifies two requirements
1	• Identifies one requirement

7) A cell is a box that is formed by the intersection of vertical and horizontal lines that divide the spreadsheet into rows and columns.

Marks	Criteria
2	• Correctly defines what a cell is
1	• Mentions one relevant point

8) Each cell is identified by the letter of the alphabet and the cell number at the point of intersection.

Marks	Criteria
1	• Correctly describes how a cell is identified

9) A value in a spreadsheet is a number or a date.

Marks	Criteria
1	• Correctly identifies a value as a number or date

10) Text is aligned to the left and values are aligned to the right in spreadsheets.

Marks	Criteria
2	• Identifies where text and values are aligned
1	• Identifies where text OR values are aligned

11) Cell formatting: can use bold; italics; underline; left, centre or right alignment; top, middle or bottom alignment; text size, colour and style; text rotation

Marks	Criteria
3	• Identifies many ways a cell can be formatted
2	• Identifies two or three ways a cell can be formatted
1	• Identifies one way a cell can be formatted

12) Currency symbols are not used in a spreadsheet because they can cause problems when using formulas.

Marks	Criteria
1	• Correctly identifies why currency symbols are not used in a spreadsheet

13) For a document to be an effective way of communication, it must be:
- Be clear, legible, concise and accurate
- Relevant, accurate, complete and up-to-date
- Meet all necessary legal requirements for documentation

Marks	Criteria
3	• Identifies three things a document must be to be an effective way of communication
2	• Identifies two things a document must be to be an effective way of communication
1	• Identifies one thing a document must be to be an effective way of communication

14) The information that most commonly is updated includes stock records; sales records; customer and supplier details; account details for customers and suppliers; technical information about products; daily, weekly or monthly sales targets and actual achievements.

Marks	Criteria
2	• Identifies a range of information that must be regularly updated
1	• Identifies type of information that must be regularly updated

15) The four most common types of formatting in Microsoft Word include:
   • Character or font formatting: including font, font size and colour
   • Paragraph formatting: includes alignment, indentation, highlighting, font type and size
   • Document or page formatting: includes spacing, margins, alignment, columns, indentation, and lists
   • Section formatting: allows you to change the page orientation or the number of columns for one section

Marks	Criteria
3	• Identifies four types of formatting in Word
2	• Identifies two or three types of formatting in Word
1	• Identifies one type of formatting in Word

16) Colour can be used in a spreadsheet for totals or to shade alternate rows.

Marks	Criteria
2	• Identifies two examples of when colour can be used in a spreadsheet
1	• Identifies one example of when colour can be used in a spreadsheet

17) Specific application functions are pre-set formulas to carry out specific calculations in a cell.

Marks	Criteria
1	• Correctly identifies a specific application function

18) Using functions is more accurate than using formulas as the margin of making mistakes is minimalised.

Marks	Criteria
1	• Correctly identifies why functions are more accurate than formulas

19) The F1 key displays the help window.

Marks	Criteria
1	• Correctly identifies what the F1 key does

Multiple choice and true/false:

1	2	3	4	5	6	7	8	9	10
d	b	d	b	c	b	a	c	c	b
11	12	13	14	15	16	17	18	19	20
c	d	b	F	T	T	T	F	T	T
21	22	23	24	25	26	27	28	29	30
F	T	T	F	F	F	T	F	T	T
31	32	33	34	35					
F	T	F	T	F					

Crossword:

The crossword solution contains the following answers:

- 1 Down: GRIDLINE
- 2 Down: FUNCTIONS
- 3 Down: QUALITYASSURANCE
- 4 Across: FINANCIALMATTERS
- 5 Down: RESSUM
- 6 Across: REALTIME
- 7 Down: OUTLOOK
- 8 Across: CELLS
- 9 Across: PARENTHESES
- 10 Down: REPUTATION
- 11 Down: CUSTOMERDATA
- 12 Across: MODIFIED
- 13 Across: FORMATTINGTOOLS
- 14 Across: LOSSOFDATA
- 15 Down: ALPHABETICAL
- 16 Across: HYPERLINKS
- 17 Across: DECIMALPOINT
- 18 Across: ROWHEADINGS
- 19 Across: SEARCHAREA
- 20 Across: SPELLING

Extended response 1:

a) Answer could include: Information and/or data is entered according to organisational requirements which are put in place to ensure compliance with laws and regulations and give guidance for decision-making and streamline internal processes. Some examples of organisational requirements are:

- Business and performance plans
- Confidentiality and security requirements
- Standards (such as for ethical behaviour) and protocols
- The vision, goals, objectives and priorities of the business
- Systems, processes and requirements for quality assurance
- Legal requirements, for example, occupational health and safety and anti-discrimination legislation

Marks	Criteria
4	• Demonstrates a sound understanding of the importance of organisational requirements for the input of data • Includes a range of examples
3	• Demonstrates a good understanding of the importance of organisational requirements for the input of data • Includes some examples
2	• Demonstrates some understanding of organisational requirements and the input of data • Includes at least one example
1	• Provides some relevant information

b) Answer could include: Large businesses may have a style guide or procedures manual which enables the business to achieve consistency and quality in its documentation. It also enables workers to efficiently produce material/documents without having to spend time thinking about style issues so management has some control over the image presented by its communications. Some requirements may include:
- Spelling, grammar, punctuation and writing style
- Document naming conventions and filing protocols
- Visual presentation, including margins, fonts and style
- Graphics standards, including the use of logos and brands

Marks	Criteria
4	• Demonstrates a sound understanding of how consistency and quality is achieved • Includes a range of examples
3	• Demonstrates a good understanding of how consistency and quality is achieved • Includes some examples
2	• Demonstrates some understanding of how consistency and quality is achieved • Includes at least one example
1	• Provides some relevant information

c) Answer could include: Formatting refers to the appearance or presentation of information or data in a software program. The way this is done will depend on the type of information or data that must be kept and the program to be used. These will also vary according to organisational and task requirements.

The four most common types of formatting in Microsoft Word include:

- Character or font formatting: determines how text, including letters, numbers, punctuation and symbols appear on the page; including font, font size and colour
- Paragraph formatting: a change in the format of text that affects an entire paragraph or is different from other paragraphs in a document; includes alignment, indentation, highlighting, font type and size
- Document or page formatting: the way a document is laid out on the page; the way it looks and is visually organised; includes font selection, font size and presentation (like bold or italics), spacing, margins, alignment, columns, indentation, and lists
- Section formatting: sections are subdivisions in a document; each section can be formatted differently; allows you to change the page orientation or the number of columns for one section

It is important that a spreadsheet is well designed so it is easy to understand. Some tips for a well-designed spreadsheet include:

- Choose a good font: Calibri 11 is a good-sized font and is the default font in Excel; do not use more than one font for the information contained in the body of the spreadsheet but a different font or size may be used for headings
- Align the data: text should be left-aligned and numbers right-aligned; if there is a lot of data to be included in one cell, use the "wrap text" option so that two lines are used for the data
- Adjust the column width and height: this gives the data "room" so it doesn't look too crowded and is easily read
- Highlight the headings: use bold capital letters and add some colour
- Use colours: do not overuse colour; use complementary colours or different shades of the same colour; good to colour the rows for totals
- Shade alternate rows for easier reading: do not use strong colours
- Don't use dark grid lines: grid lines put too much emphasis on each individual cell so should be used sparingly; can use solid lines for row borders and dotted lines for column borders; if shading every second row, only include column borders

Marks	Criteria
6-7	• Demonstrates a extensive knowledge of formatting
4-5	• Demonstrates a thorough knowledge of formatting
2-3	• Demonstrates some knowledge of formatting
1	• Provides some relevant information

Extended response 2:

Marks	Criteria
13-15	• Demonstrates an extensive knowledge and understanding of organisational requirements • Clearly explains the relationship between organisational requirements and the processing of information or data • Communicates ideas and information using relevant workplace examples and industry terminology • Presents a logical and cohesive response
10-12	• Demonstrates a sound knowledge and understanding of organisational requirements • Explains the relationship between organisational requirements and the processing of information or data • Communicates using relevant workplace examples and industry terminology • Presents a logical response
7-9	• Demonstrates some knowledge and understanding of organisational requirements • Shows some relationship between organisational requirements and the processing of information or data • Communicates using some workplace examples and industry terminology • Demonstrates some organisation in presenting information
4-6	• Demonstrates basic knowledge and/or understanding of organisational requirements AND/OR processing of information or data • Uses some industry terminology
1-3	• Provides some relevant information

Answer could include:
- Definition of organisational requirements
- Why organisational requirements are put in place
- Examples of organisational requirements that affect the processing of information or data in documents
- Examples of how documents can be changed in appearance due to organisational requirements

Chapter 3:

1. All documents are checked for spelling, grammar and formatting mistakes as well as accuracy of facts.

Marks	Criteria
2	• Identifies a range of items that are checked for accuracy
1	• Identifies one item that is checked for accuracy

2. You should not just rely on auto spell check as some words are spelt differently in Australia compared to the default settings of the program being used.

Marks	Criteria
2	• Detailed explanation why you shouldn't just rely on auto spell check
1	• Brief explanation why you shouldn't just rely on auto spell check

3. The format of the whole document should be reviewed to check that it flows logically from one section to the next and that headings etc are consistent throughout.

Marks	Criteria
2	• Identifies two or more reasons why the format of the whole document should be reviewed
1	• Identifies one reason why the format of the whole document should be reviewed

4. Factual information is essential to the reputation of the business.

Marks	Criteria
1	• Identifies why factual information is essential

5. Metadata includes identifying information such as your initials, full name or business name as well as more personal information such as your computer and hard drive names, hidden data in cells and comments you placed in the spreadsheet.

Marks	Criteria
2	• Detailed explanation of metadata
1	• Mentions one relevant point

6. Metadata can be removed by:
   - Click the "File" tab, select "Info" and then click the "Check for Issues" icon
   - Select "Inspect Document" from the list
   - Check each box to include all types of metadata in the inspection and click "Inspect"
   - Review the results of the inspection in the Document Inspector dialog box
   - Click the "Remove All" button next to each metadata category to delete it from the document

Marks	Criteria
2	• Detailed explanation of how metadata can be deleted
1	• Mentions one relevant point

7. A file is an organised unit of documents dealing with the same subject, activity or transaction.

Marks	Criteria
2	• Detailed definition of a file
1	• Mentions one relevant point

8. Files can be stored in a paper-based system in a filing cabinet or electronically on a computer.

Marks	Criteria
2	• Identifies two methods of filing
1	• Identifies one method of filing

9. The following should be recorded on the front of a paper-based file:

   - File reference number
   - File title
   - Date opened
   - Date closed (if applicable)
   - The name of the person responsible for the file
   - Department or team name

Marks	Criteria
2	• Identifies a range of information that should be recorded on the front of a paper-based file
1	• Identifies one piece of information that should be recorded on the front of a paper-based file

9. Electronic files can be stored alphabetically, alpha-numerically, chronologically, geographically, numerically or by subject.

Marks	Criteria
2	• Identifies a range of ways electronic files can be stored
1	• Identifies one way an electronic file can be stored

10. Folders can be filed by the type of product, names of clients, geographical areas, time spans (week, month or year) or type of action (invoices, statements, letters).

Marks	Criteria
2	• Identifies a range of ways folders can be filed
1	• Identifies one way a folder can be filed

11. A File Naming Convention is a framework for naming files in a way that describes what they contain and how they relate to other files.

Marks	Criteria
2	• Detailed definition of a File Naming Convention
1	• Mentions one relevant point

12. A 'revision' numbering system: any major changes to a file can be indicated by whole numbers, for example, v01 would be the first version, v02 the second version etc; minor changes can be indicated by increasing the decimal figure, for example, v01_01 indicates a minor change has been made to the first version, and v03_01 a minor change has been made to the third version.

Marks	Criteria
2	• Detailed explanation of a revision numbering system
1	• Mentions one relevant point

13. "copy" should be included in the name of the file when it is downloaded from the server and "saved as" on an individual's computer.

Marks	Criteria
2	• Detailed explanation of when "copy" should be included in the name of a file
1	• Mentions one relevant point

14. When starting a new document, it is a good idea to name it and save it before you start entering text.

Marks	Criteria
1	• Identifies what you should do when starting a new document.

15. Every few minutes you should save the document, so if anything unpredicted should happen (like a power outage), you would lose very little work.

Marks	Criteria
1	• Identifies why you should save a document every few minutes

Multiple choice and true/false:

1	2	3	4	5	6	7	8	9	10
c	b	c	c	a	b	d	d	b	c
11	12	13	14	15	16	17	18	19	20
F	T	F	T	F	F	T	T	F	T
21	22	23	24	25	26	27	28	29	30
T	T	T	F	F	T	T	T	F	F
31	32	33	34	35					
F	T	T	T	T					

Crossword:

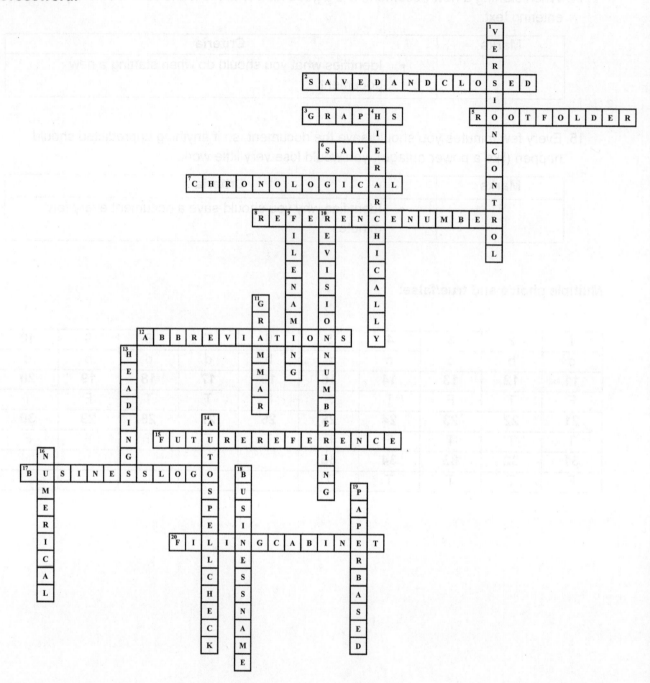

Across:
2. SAVEDANDCLOSED
3. GRAPHS
5. ROOTFOLDER
6. SAVE
7. CHRONOLOGICAL
8. REFERENCENUMBER
12. ABBREVIATIONS
15. FUTUREREFERENCE
17. BUSINESSLOGO
20. FILINGCABINET

Down:
1. VERSIONCONTROL
4. HIERARCHICALLY
9. FILENAME
10. REVISIONNUMBERING
11. GRMMMAR
13. HEADING
14. AUTOSPELLCHECK
16. NUMERICAL
18. BUSINESSNAME
19. PAPERBASED

Extended response 1:

a) Answer could include: When proofreading a document, you should always:

- Check that the tone and style and the purpose of the document match the organisational and task requirements. Sentences should not be too long and be written in a tone to suit the intended audience.
- Review the format of the whole document, checking that it flows logically from one section to the next and that headings etc are consistent throughout.
- Check spelling and grammar rather than just relying on auto spell check as some words are spelt differently in Australia compared to the default settings of the program being used.
- Review the overall layout of the whole document, especially at consistency for margins, alignment and justification. Also check that charts, graphs and pictures are formatted correctly and placed in a position that doesn't overwhelm the text.
- Check that the business logo is in the correct position and adheres to organisational requirements as to placement and presentation.
- Check that all information is factual as this is essential to the reputation of the business.

Marks	Criteria
4	• Demonstrates a sound understanding of proofreading • Includes a range of examples
3	• Demonstrates a good understanding of proofreading • Includes some examples
2	• Demonstrates some understanding of proofreading • Includes at least one example
1	• Provides some relevant information

b) Answer could include: Metadata should be removed before being shared with other people or the general public, in order to maintain privacy. To do this, you must:

- Click the "File" tab, select "Info" and then click the "Check for Issues" icon
- Select "Inspect Document" from the list
- Check each box to include all types of metadata in the inspection and click "Inspect"
- Review the results of the inspection in the Document Inspector dialog box
- Click the "Remove All" button next to each metadata category to delete it from the document

Marks	Criteria
4	• Demonstrates a sound understanding of metadata • Includes a range of examples
3	• Demonstrates a good understanding of metadata • Includes some examples
2	• Demonstrates some understanding of metadata • Includes at least one example
1	• Provides some relevant information

c) Answer could include:

Every business has its own system of naming and storing files. Generally, all files about a particular topic are grouped in one folder so they are located together for easy access. Folders should be named according to the area of work they relate to. This could include naming folders by the type of product, names of clients, geographical areas, time spans (week, month or year) or type of action (invoices, statements, letters).

In a paper-based filing system, the following information should always be provided on the cover of each file:

- File reference number
- File title
- Date opened
- Date closed (if applicable)
- The name of the person responsible for the file
- Department or team name

Electronic files are stored on computer systems. Microsoft Access or Works store databases, Microsoft Word or Excel store various documents and spreadsheets while emails are stored in Yahoo or Hotmail etc. Methods for classifying files include:

- Alphabetical: filing under the names of clients, patients or customers in alphabetical order from A to Z (titles like Mr & Mrs should be disregarded; hyphenated names should be treated as one name)
- Alpha-numerical: combination of letters and numbers, with letters stated first
- Chronological: often used in conjunction with other filing methods and involves sorting records according to their date, with the most recent on top
- Geographical: usually filed alphabetically according to geographical location like a state, city, town or suburb
- Numerical: filed in order from low to high; should always be cross-referenced to an alphabetical list; used for systems where many files will be added in time as numbers are infinite (like patient records in a hospital)
- By subject: filed alphabetically according to the subject matter

A new File Naming Convention (FNC) should be chosen when creating a new document. A File Naming Convention is a framework for naming files in a way that describes what they contain and how they relate to other files. The FNC should be consistent, meaningful to all workers and be easily accessed when needed.

A 'revision' numbering system should be used. Any major changes to a file can be indicated by whole numbers, for example, v01 would be the first version, v02 the second version etc; minor changes can be indicated by increasing the decimal figure, for example, v01_01 indicates a minor change has been made to the first version, and v03_01 a minor change has been made to the third version.

Marks	Criteria
6-7	• Demonstrates a extensive knowledge of naming and filing documents
4-5	• Demonstrates a thorough knowledge of naming and filing documents
2-3	• Demonstrates some knowledge of naming and filing documents
1	• Provides some relevant information

Extended response 2:

Answer should include an explanation of the following:
- The process of proofreading
- The removal of metadata from spreadsheets
- Paper-based v electronic filing systems
- How files should be named and stored
- How these processes are affected by organisational and task requirements

Marks	Criteria
13-15	• Demonstrates an extensive knowledge and understanding of reviewing data and preparing it for storage • Clearly explains the relationship between organisational and task requirements and reviewing and storing data • Communicates ideas and information using relevant workplace examples and industry terminology • Presents a logical and cohesive response
10-12	• Demonstrates a sound knowledge and understanding of reviewing data and preparing it for storage • Explains the relationship between organisational and task requirements and reviewing and storing data • Communicates using relevant workplace examples and industry terminology • Presents a logical response
7-9	• Demonstrates some knowledge and understanding of reviewing data and preparing it for storage • Shows some relationship between organisational requirements and the processing of information or data • Communicates using some workplace examples and industry terminology • Demonstrates some organisation in presenting information
4-6	• Demonstrates basic knowledge and/or understanding of organisational and task requirements AND/OR reviewing data and preparing it for storage • Uses some industry terminology
1-3	• Provides some relevant information

Chapter 4:

Note: These tasks are not awarded marks. Submitted answers will be marked as competent or not yet competent. Any task that is deemed not yet competent must be reviewed, updated and resubmitted until it has been deemed competent. Record the date when deemed competent.

Task	Competent	Not yet competent
Northern Beaches Bike Tours: Exercise 1		
Northern Beaches Bike Tours: Exercise 2		
Northern Beaches Bike Tours: Exercise 3		
Northern Beaches Bike Tours: Exercise 4		
Northern Beaches Bike Tours: Exercise 5		
Northern Beaches Bike Tours: Exercise 6		
Northern Beaches Bike Tours: Exercise 7		
Northern Beaches Bike Tours: Exercise 8		
Northern Beaches Bike Tours: Exercise 9		
Northern Beaches Bike Tours: Exercise 10		
Northern Beaches Bike Tours: Exercise 11		
Northern Beaches Bike Tours: Exercise 12		
Northern Beaches Bike Tours: Exercise 13		
Task 1		

Notes